Landmarks of world literature

Thomas Hardy

TESS OF THE D'URBERVILL

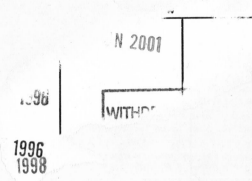

Landmarks of world literature

General Editor: J. P. Stern

THOMAS HARDY

Tess of the d'Urbervilles

DALE KRAMER

University of Illinois at Urbana–Champaign

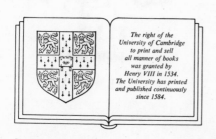

The right of the
University of Cambridge
to print and sell
all manner of books
was granted by
Henry VIII in 1534.
The University has printed
and published continuously
since 1584.

CAMBRIDGE UNIVERSITY PRESS

Cambridge

New York   Port Chester   Melbourne   Sydney

Published by the Press Syndicate of the University of Cambridge
The Pitt Building, Trumpington Street, Cambridge CB2 1RP
40 West 20th Street, New York, NY 10011-4211, USA
10 Stamford Road, Oakleigh, Melbourne 3166, Australia

© Cambridge University Press 1991

First published 1991

Printed in Great Britain at the University Press, Cambridge

British Library cataloguing in publication data
Kramer, Dale *1936–*
Thomas Hardy: Tess of the d'Urbervilles. – (Landmarks of
world literature).
1. Fiction in English. Hardy, Thomas, 1840–1928
I. Title   II. Series
823.8

Library of Congress cataloguing in publication data
Kramer, Dale, 1936–
Thomas Hardy, Tess of the d'Urbervilles / Dale Kramer.
    p.   cm. – (Landmarks of world literature)
Includes bibliographical references.
ISBN 0 521 34627 4. – ISBN 0 521 34695 9 (pbk.)
1. Hardy, Thomas, 1840–1928. Tess of the d'Urbervilles.
I. Title.   II. Series.
PR4748.K7   1991
823'.8 – dc20   90–26322   CIP

ISBN 0 521 34627 4 hardback
ISBN 0 521 34695 9 paperback

Contents

Text and acknowledgements

Many editions of Hardy's novels exist, most of them based on the 1912 Wessex Edition (Macmillan), the last edition published in his lifetime for which he both furnished printer's copy and corrected the galleys. The edition from which passages are quoted is the Oxford World's Classics Edition, edited by Simon Gatrell (1988), which is a corrected reprint of the Clarendon text of the novel edited by Juliet Grindle and Simon Gatrell (Oxford: Clarendon Press, 1983). For ease in locating the cited material in other editions of *Tess*, I give chapter numbers, as well as page numbers from the World's Classics Edition.

This book has been much improved by the discriminating attention, careful eye, and pencil of Peter Stern. Nancy Marck did an excellent job with the initial stages of the biographical, literary, and historical charts. One sentence in 'Plot' was suggested by Joseph Carroll after reading a shorter version of these ideas. A few phrases and sentences in the section named 'Tess' are rewritten from my *Thomas Hardy: The Forms of Tragedy* (London: Macmillan, 1975).

Chronology

	Hardy's life and works	Related literary events	Related historical events
1830			Liverpool to Manchester railway line opens, marking the beginning of the railway era.
1833			'Tolpuddle Martyrs' case: Dorset agricultural labourers' attempt to unionise fails.
1837			
1840	Thomas Hardy born 2 June, Higher Bockhampton, Dorset, first child of Thomas and Jemima Hardy (née Hand).		Victoria is crowned Queen of England.
1842			Working-class agitation reaches its peak in the Chartist riots.
1844			England's first telegraph line constructed.
1846			Potato famine in Ireland; Corn Laws repealed, allowing the importation of foreign grain.
1847		C. Brontë, *Jane Eyre*; E. Brontë, *Wuthering Heights*.	Railway arrives in Dorchester.

1848–56	Attends various schools, including the National School (Church of England) in Bockhampton; the British School in Greyhound Yard, Dorchester, run by Isaac Glandfield Last; and an independent school for older students, also run by Last.	Gaskell, *Mary Barton* (1848); C. Brontë, *Shirley* (1849); Tennyson becomes poet laureate; *In Memoriam*; Hawthorne, *The Scarlet Letter* (1850); Arnold, *Poems* (1853); Dickens, *Hard Times* (1854); Gaskell, *North and South*; Browning, *Men and Women*; Trollope, *The Warden* (1855); Flaubert, *Madame Bovary* (1856).	Public Health Act (1848) passed in response to chronic cholera epidemics; Great Exhibition opens in Hyde Park (1851), focusing the world's attention on England's material progress; Crimean War (1854–56).
1856–64	Articled to John Hicks, a Dorchester architect, for four years, then employed by Hicks as architect's clerk.		
1857		Eliot, *Scenes of Clerical Life*; E. B. Browning, *Aurora Leigh*.	Matrimonial Causes Act establishes divorce courts.
1859		Darwin, *Origin of Species*; Eliot, *Adam Bede*; Meredith, *The Ordeal of Richard Feverel*; Mill, *On Liberty*.	
1860		Eliot, *The Mill on the Floss*; Dickens, *Great Expectations*.	
1861			American Civil War begins. Death of Prince Albert (Queen Victoria's consort).
1862	Assistant architect in London.	Meredith, *Modern Love*; Victor Hugo, *Les Misérables*.	

	Hardy's life and works	Related literary events	Related historical events
1863	Awarded prize for architecture, but denied a cash prize. Becomes engaged to Eliza Bright Nicholls, a lady's maid in London.	Huxley, *Man's Place in Nature*; Tolstoy begins *War and Peace*.	
1864		Browning, *Dramatis Personae*; Newman, *Apologia pro Vita Sua*.	
1865	Publishes a prose sketch in *Chambers's Journal*, winning his first money as a writer.	Swinburne, *Atalanta in Calydon*; Arnold, *Essays in Criticism* I.	
1866	Abandons ambition to attend university and enter the Church.	Eliot, *Felix Holt*; Swinburne, *Poems and Ballads*; Ibsen, *Brand*; Dostoevsky, *Crime and Punishment*.	The Hyde Park Riots express the demand for electoral reform.
1867	Suffering from ill health, Hardy returns to Bockhampton and employment with Hicks. Breaks his engagement with Eliza Nicholls.	Arnold, *New Poems*, *Culture and Anarchy*; Ibsen, *Peer Gynt*; Trollope, *The Last Chronicle of Barset*.	Under Derby's Conservative administration, the Second Reform Bill grants the vote to the urban working class.
1868	Sends MS of first novel, *The Poor Man and the Lady*, to the publisher Alexander Macmillan, who rejects the novel but offers encouraging advice, as does his reader, George Meredith. Although no copy of this novel remains, ideas and sections from it appear in later novels.	Browning, *The Ring and the Book*; Dostoevsky, *The Idiot*.	Public executions abolished.
1869	John Hicks dies. Hardy moves to Weymouth to work, also begins writing *Desperate Remedies*.	Mill, *The Subjection of Women*; Blackmore, *Lorna Doone*.	Contagious Diseases Act passed, subjecting female prostitutes to police and medical registration. First women's college established at Cambridge (Girton).

Year	Hardy's life	Literary context	Historical context
1870	Macmillan rejects *Desperate Remedies*; William Tinsley agrees to publish it on receipt of £75 from Hardy. Hardy meets and becomes engaged to Emma Lavinia Gifford while planning the restoration of a church in St Juliot, Cornwall.		Education Act institutes the first national school system, attendance compulsory up to age thirteen. The first Married Women's Property Act gives women the right to retain possession of money they earn.
1871	*Desperate Remedies* published, to mixed reviews. Offers manuscript of *Under the Greenwood Tree* to Macmillan, who suggests Hardy resubmit it early in the next year. Hardy instead sells it to Tinsley, who publishes it in 1872, to generally favourable reviews.	Darwin, *The Descent of Man*; Eliot, *Middlemarch*; Swinburne, *Songs Before Sunrise*.	Abolition of religious tests at universities. Trade unions legalised.
1873	*A Pair of Blue Eyes*, Hardy's first novel to be published under his name, receives positive reviews. Hardy's friend Horace Moule commits suicide in his Cambridge rooms.	Pater, *Studies in the History of the Renaissance*; Mill, *Autobiography*; Tolstoy begins *Anna Karenina*; John Addington Symonds, *Studies of the Greek Poets*.	Beginning of agricultural depression and decline that continues into the twentieth century.
1874	*Far from the Madding Crowd* serialised in *Cornhill Magazine* and published as a book. Marries Emma Gifford on 17 September.		
1875	First published poem, 'The Fire at Tranter Sweatley's', in *Gentleman's Magazine*.	Trollope, *The Way We Live Now*.	

	Hardy's life and works	Related literary events	Related historical events
1876	*The Hand of Ethelberta* published. The Hardys move to Sturminster Newton, north Dorset.	Eliot, *Daniel Deronda*; Meredith, *Beauchamp's Career*.	
1877		Meredith, *An Essay on Comedy*; Zola, *L'Assommoir*.	Society for the Protection of Ancient Buildings founded.
1878	*The Return of the Native* published. Emma's social aspirations bring the Hardys back to London, to the suburb of Tooting.		
1879	*New Quarterly Magazine* publishes two short stories, 'The Distracted Young Preacher' and 'Fellow–Townsmen'.	Meredith, *The Egoist*; Ibsen, *A Doll's House*; Dostoevsky, *The Brothers Karamazov*.	Disraeli refuses protective tariffs for British farmers.
1880	*The Trumpet–Major* published. Hardy falls ill during the writing of *A Laodicean*. While bedridden, he dictates the rest of *A Laodicean* to Emma. Without Emma's consent, Thomas decides to build a home in Dorchester.	Gissing, *Workers in the Dawn*; Zola, *Nana*.	
1881	The Hardys move to Wimbourne for Thomas's health.	James, *Portrait of a Lady*; Ibsen, *Ghosts*; Anatole France, *Le Crime de Sylvestre Bonnard*.	Social Democratic Federation formed.
1882	*Two on a Tower* published, and criticised for its immorality.	Stevenson, *Treasure Island*; Jefferies, *Bevis*.	The second Married Women's Property Act secures for married women the right to separate ownership of property.
1883	The Hardys move to Shire–Hall Place in Dorchester.	Olive Schreiner, *The Story of an African Farm*.	

Year	Hardy's life and works	Literary context	Historical and cultural background
1884	Appointed a Justice of the Peace for the Borough of Dorchester. Joins local antiquarian societies and becomes friendly with local gentry. Thomas and Emma move into Max Gate in June.		Under Liberal Prime Minister Gladstone, the Third Reform Bill grants agricultural workers the right to vote.
1885		Ibsen, *Wild Duck*. Meredith, *Diana of the Crossways*; Pater, *Marius the Epicurean*; Howells, *The Rise of Silas Lapham*; Zola, *Germinal*.	
1886	*The Mayor of Casterbridge* published.	Stevenson, *Dr. Jekyll and Mr. Hyde*; Gissing, *Demos*; Ibsen, *Rosmersholm*. Jefferies, *Amaryllis at the Fair*.	Gladstone's Irish Home Rule Bill defeated in the Commons. 'Bloody Sunday' demonstrations in Trafalgar Square.
1887	*The Woodlanders* published.		
1888	*Wessex Tales* (short stories) published, as is the essay 'The Profitable Reading of Fiction'.	Mrs Humphrey Ward, *Robert Elsmere*.	
1889	Hardy meets Agatha (Mrs Hamo) Thornycroft, who may have been the physical model for Tess Durbeyfield. Tillotson's newspaper syndicate refuses to publish *Tess* after Hardy declines to make requested changes.	Pater, *Appreciations*.	London Dock Strike, the most famous of many industrial actions.
1890	'Candour in English Fiction' published as part of a symposium in the *New Review*.	Frazer, *The Golden Bough*; A. France, *Thaïs*.	USA Copyright Act, granting authors of other countries control over and income from US editions of their works. *Tess* came under this protection by a matter of weeks.

	Hardy's life and works	Related literary events	Related historical events
1891	'The Science of Fiction' published in the *New Review. A Group of Noble Dames* (short stories) published. *Tess* published by Osgood, McIlvaine; reviews are split, but more in favour than against.	Gissing, *New Grub Street*; Wilde, *The Picture of Dorian Gray*.	
1892	*The Pursuit of the Well-Beloved* published as serial; the thinly veiled exploration of Hardy's dissatisfaction with his marriage causes further deterioration of his relationship with Emma.	Ibsen, *Master Builder*; Zola, *La Débâcle*; George Egerton, *Keynotes*.	
1893	Meets and is immediately attracted to Florence Henniker, author of three novels and wife of Arthur Henry Henniker-Major, on a trip to Ireland with Emma.	Sarah Grand, *The Heavenly Twins*.	Independent Labour Party formed.
1894	Begins extensive revisions of his novels for the 'Wessex Novels' edition (Osgood, McIlvaine).	Kipling, *The Jungle Book*; Shaw, *Arms and the Man*; Moore, *Esther Waters*; Egerton, *Discords*.	
1895	Diluted version of *Jude* published serially. The book edition arouses much hostility. The first maps of Hardy's fictional Wessex printed. The Hardys' marriage continues to deteriorate. Emma becomes more involved in various humanitarian and feminist causes; her attempts to publish her own literary works are unsuccessful.	Wells, *The Time Machine*; Wilde, *The Importance of Being Earnest*; Grant Allen, *The Woman Who Did*.	

1896	The Hardys travel in England and Belgium, revisiting their honeymoon hotel without reviving original feelings.	
1897	*The Pursuit of the Well-Beloved* published in book form. Critics not happy with its sexual theme despite revisions. Determined to write no more novels, Hardy begins to gather poems for a book.	Conrad, *The Nigger of the 'Narcissus'*.
1898	*Wessex Poems and Other Verses* published, to the amazement of readers and critics. Reviews are mixed; Hardy resents being labelled a pessimist. Emma responds negatively. She moves into garret rooms in Max Gate, both to work and to sleep.	
1899	Hardy responds to the strife in South Africa through a series of poems published in national newspapers.	Conrad, *Lord Jim*. The Boer War begins, splitting England domestically into pro- and anti-war factions.
1900		
1901	*Poems of the Past and the Present* published, to great critical acclaim.	Queen Victoria dies; Edward VII succeeds.

	Hardy's life and works	Related literary events	Related historical events
1902			The Boer War ends.
1903		James, *The Ambassadors*.	
1904	Part First of *The Dynasts* published. Reviewers puzzled by both form and style. Jemima Hardy dies on 3 April. Emma does not attend the funeral.		
1905	Honorary Doctorate of Laws (University of Aberdeen). Meets Florence Emily Dugdale, a teacher and author of children's books.		
1906, 1908	Parts Second and Third of *The Dynasts* published, to increasing critical approval.	Galsworthy, *The Man of Property* (1906); Bennett, *The Old Wives' Tale* (1908).	Women's Freedom League established (1908).
1909	Hardy and Emma attend the first night of Baron Frederick d'Erlanger's opera *Tess*, not noted for its fidelity to Hardy's novel. *Time's Laughingstocks* published.		
1910	Florence Dugdale and Emma begin a close friendship. Hardy receives Order of Merit (June); freedom of the Borough of Dorchester (November).	Forster, *Howards End*.	King Edward VII dies; George V succeeds.
1911	Makes final revisions in most of his novels, for the Wessex Edition (published by Macmillan in 1912).		

Year			
1912	Receives gold medal from the Royal Society of Literature. Her health declining, Emma publishes *Spaces*, a prose volume describing her religious beliefs. Emma dies on 27 November.		
1913	Deliberate immersion in memories and associated emotions of his earliest times with Emma results in an intensely productive period of writing poetry.	Lawrence, *Sons and Lovers*.	
1914	6 February, Thomas Hardy and Florence Dugdale are married. *Satires of Circumstances* published. Hardy depressed by First World War, more so when Frank George, a distant cousin he was considering as his heir, dies at Gallipoli.	Joyce, *Dubliners*.	First World War begins.
1915		Woolf, *The Voyage Out*.	
1916			Easter uprising in Dublin.
1917	*Moments of Vision* published. Begins working on the autobiographical narratives that were published posthumously as biographies by Florence.		
1918			First World War ends. Women over thirty who are householders or married to householders get the vote.
1920	Honorary D. Litt. from Oxford.		

	Hardy's life and works	Related literary events
1922	Florence and Thomas finish his 'biography'. Honorary fellowship from The Queen's College, Oxford.	Woolf, *Jacob's Room*; Joyce, *Ulysses*.
1923	Hardy's old friend and object of romantic interest, Florence Henniker, dies.	
1924	Hardy becomes involved in a new dramatic adaptation of *Tess*. His growing interest in local actress Gertrude Bugler, who plays Tess, moves Florence to persuade Bugler not to perform in the London production planned for the next year.	Forster, *A Passage to India*.
1925	Successful London production of *Tess*, with another actress in the title role. *Human Shows, Far Phantasies: Songs, and Trifles* published.	Woolf, *Mrs. Dalloway*.
1927	11 January, Thomas Hardy dies after several weeks of illness. His body is cremated and buried in Westminster Abbey, while his heart is buried in Stinsford Churchyard in Emma's grave. *Winter Words* published posthumously.	Woolf, *To the Lighthouse*.
1928	*The Early Life of Thomas Hardy* published.	
1930	*The Later Years of Thomas Hardy* published.	
1937	17 October, Florence Hardy dies of cancer.	

Chapter 1

Introduction

'Yet there was nothing ethereal about it [Tess's face]: all was real vitality, real warmth, real incarnation' (*Tess of the d'Urbervilles* 24: 152). 'There was hardly a touch of earth in her love for Clare' (31: 193). In these two passages is compressed one of the central factors of the appeal of *Tess of the d'Urbervilles*: Hardy simultaneously − or rather, perhaps, alternately − suggests that life is characterised by ethereality or abstract values and emphasises the daunting rigour of maintaining life. He accompanies the view of an elevated mentalist, even idealist, existence with the contrasting force of substantiality, reality as it is commonly understood, without even hinting that these moods or perceptions might cancel out the other's absolutism. Similar oppositions − Angel vs Alec, conventional morality vs nature, love vs sexuality, grand past vs hardscrabble present, morality vs exploitation − organise the novel. Without directly evaluating these oppositions, Hardy firmly refuses to attempt to restrict the validity (or weakness) of one of the polar forces by the existence of the other. Moreover, in the course of the novel − even towards the end − Tess moves frequently from generalised tragic stature and insight into mundane, limited, local pragmatic reaction, underscoring the uncertainty that is at the centre of the novel's permanent appeal.

Embodying such contrasts, *Tess* superbly represents Hardy's incorporation of forces operative in himself and his society towards the end of the nineteenth century in Britain. His other works develop aspects of the views present in *Tess of the d'Urbervilles*, but it is as if his earlier works were trial employments of various devices and subject matter, and juxtapositions of attitudes and ambitions. Although his achievement may be 'finer' or more finished in other novels (one thinks of *The Mayor of Casterbridge* in particular), *Tess* is Hardy's richest and most ambitious story, the one which tested his mastery of his subject matter and technique. That this is a marred novel only indicates the strain of co-ordinating all of his materials.

Tess of the d'Urbervilles is one of the nineteenth century's great texts of democracy, its ineffable message all the more striking and powerful for its being encased in a highly sophisticated medium that may look to the unpractised, callow eye to be roughshod and even crude. The message involving a substructure of politics is all the more devious for the novel's surface seeming to be a diatribe against a reigning current ideology, Victorian hypocrisy. *Tess of the d'Urbervilles* is a landmark volume because it is its author's most comprehensive expression of a message he presented elsewhere with perhaps finer artistry, but artistry on a smaller scale precisely because he could not put all the message into another narrative. He had in other stories been a political radical, before *Tess* and after he experimented in fine aesthetic effects (*The Woodlanders*, perhaps *The Well-Beloved*); but in no other novel was he able to employ the pedantry of a self-taught devotee of Greek classics, the grim knowledge of a rural youth who had seen the corpse of a starved eighteen-year-old boy whose stomach, he learned later, contained nothing but turnips; the artistic skills of a man who had written novels in several tones. *Tess* is at once profoundly rebellious and destructive of its society's abiding belief systems, while in other ways it underscores the validity of that belief system (sometimes through expressions revealing the artist's biases in ways he probably would not have appreciated himself).

Tess of the d'Urbervilles is volume I of the Wessex Novels, Hardy's first collected edition (1895), and of the Wessex Edition (1912), the last edition which he prepared for the press. Thomas Hardy recognised its primacy among his works. Already respected as a serious novelist before 1890, with the appearance of *Tess* he was elevated to the level of George Meredith as a novelist of permanent importance. In classing it among his 'Novels of Character and Environment', he put it with those books on which his modern reputation as a writer of fiction solidly rests – *Under the Greenwood Tree, Far from the Madding Crowd, The Return of the Native, The Mayor of Casterbridge, The Woodlanders, Wessex Tales, Life's Little Ironies,* and *Jude the Obscure.* Any one of five of the novels in this group would warrant inclusion in the present Landmarks series had Hardy not written *Tess. Tess* shares many qualities and characteristics of these, yet by general judgement has greater interest than any other of Hardy's works.

Beyond question, it is Hardy's most varied and rewarding novel, although of his five or six great novels it is also one of the least polished. There are elements of inchoateness in the novel, some brought about by revisions Hardy made in certain passages that conflict with other passages he left unchanged. Contributing to the inchoateness (which is not extreme) and uncertainty more than incomplete revisions, however, is that the very nature of Tess's personality, and her situation as developed in the novel, convey a sense of profound authorial involvement beyond that in any other of Hardy's novels, an engagement that is intellectual as well as emotional.

Thinking and writing about tragedy is also necessary in a book on *Tess,* because after the traditional concept of tragedy used in *The Mayor of Casterbridge* Hardy began – I think it cannot be doubted – to experiment with other concepts, as if in search of a form appropriate for the issues and types of characters and dilemmas he was concerned with.

The linear narrative contributes powerfully to the novel's impact as tragedy, as it traces the disastrous course of its protagonist. It opens with Tess dressed in white at a May dance, at which her future husband, Angel Clare, on a walking tour with his brothers, stops to see the rustic ritual. Ironically, however, he does not dance with her, and this mischance typifies Tess's experiences, what Hardy calls concatenations of circumstance. Her father drinks too much that night, because he has just learned his Durbeyfield family are descendants of the medieval d'Urberville knights, and so she replaces him in his carter's role of hauling sales products to market; but, falling asleep on the way, she feels responsible for the death of the family's horse, struck in the dark by a mail-cart. To make up for their loss, she goes to work for Alec Stokes, whose businessman father had retired and taken the name of the supposedly extinct d'Urbervilles, and who she assumes is her relative. He seduces her — or rapes her, the distinction being one of the novel's unresolvable points. Although she considers herself unworthy because of her relationship with Alec, she is unable to resist her love for Angel, whom she meets at the dairy she goes to work at after her baby dies and after she has begun to recover her joy of living. Wanting to be honest with him, she writes Angel a note that he does not see; so she confesses to him her past only on their wedding night, after he has confessed a similar premarital sexual relationship. This is the crucial event of her life, because Angel — although thinking himself an enlightened man who has rejected society, sophistication, religious hypocrisy, and materialism for a rural retreat — is so conventional concerning sex that he cannot bear to live in the same country with Tess and her still-living former lover. He emigrates to Brazil. He thinks that he has left Tess enough money to live on in his absence, but he has not taken into account his wife's sense of responsibility for her family. Impoverished by their hapless ways, she is forced to return to Alec, shortly before Angel, finally made repentant, returns. To be able to have Angel's love, if only briefly, Tess kills Alec. Her execution follows speedily.

An aspect of the power of *Tess* not easy to identify securely from this sketch is the precise nature of its appeal at the level of myth: that is, its appeal that goes beyond the temporal, historical, societally relevant. I hazard that it is the figure of Tess herself, as the hyper-suffering and hyper-put-upon human figure, who, having lost everything (including religious belief), finally takes vengeance on her most obvious oppressor. Such objections as that Tess need not kill Alec, she can merely leave him and justify herself to Angel (an action Hardy prepares the reader for but fails to give any indications of to Tess); that her return to Alec as his lover is gratuitous since he had promised reparation to her family for his previous seduction of her; that Tess disappoints aesthetically and morally because

Angel is not worthy of her − these objections fade away in face of the directness and irreversibility of the only forceful action she takes in the entire novel, and which parallels the pain she has been made to suffer at the hands of others.

Chapter 2

Backgrounds

Hardy is frequently characterised as an autodidact, which could lead one to expect that his work displays the impact of his reading and of models in a manner different from the work of an author embodying more complex relations of 'raw living', cognition, and aesthetics. With most writers with a conventional education, predecessors and competitors are mediated by tutors, lecturers, experiences in the classroom, experiences involving other students of similar age. Hardy did not lack group education totally. He attended briefly the Stinsford National School and spent three years in each of two schools in Dorchester, the British School and a commercial academy. Obviously, the number and range of topics a young student would customarily cover over a longer number of years in group or formal surroundings exceeded Hardy's experience. None the less, by the standards of his time, his education was not especially stinted. He was not as self-taught, nor as isolated from guidance, as the term autodidact implies. But his significant education was self-directed and adventitious. He learned Latin and a little Greek on his own. Eagerness to learn and personal interchange made up for and perhaps was more effective than rote study. While working in the office of a Dorchester architect, Hardy and Henry Bastow discussed the Greek of the New Testament, while outside the office he and Horace Moule discussed literary subjects. And he was a wide and eager reader all of his life. Even if it is true that he did not read Schopenhauer until late in his career (*World as Will and Idea* was not translated into English until 1886), he could have learned of Schopenhauer's central ideas in any of the many explications of current philosophical controversies which were the frequent subjects of essays in Victorian periodicals. The recent publication of Hardy's literary notebooks makes generally available the evidence that Hardy read in Greek drama, Victorian political and economic writers, and philosophers (Björk).

What I would like to explore here briefly are a few aspects of the background of Hardy's life and work which have not been unrecognised but which have been less explored than others. That is, the impact of Schopenhauer has been early and well demonstrated by Helen Garwood in 1909–11, subsequent students wrangling over extent and origin of the similarities in the ideas of the philosophy and the novelist – poet. By saying little about such as John Stuart Mill and Charles Darwin, I do not mean to suggest their unimportance, but to acknowledge that these influences are well known, and ideas about them can be gained by reading existing scholarship, some of which I cite in the Further Reading section. Also, much of the impact upon Hardy of so-called influences is tangential. Or, at least, that is how I interpret the frequent impression given by allusions to the sorts of knowledge one would ordinarily gain in school, and which Hardy gained by determination and self-discipline. That is, they seem to be imposed upon the passages in which they appear, as if their author felt the need to buttress a perception of his own by force of authority of its bearing upon a classical situation or image. Thus, for example, in *The Return of the Native* he defends Eustacia as 'Queen of Night' by comparing her to Bathsheba, Saul, and several other great figures of myth and history.

People do not read Hardy for such allusions, I think; instead, his characterising traits reflect his bond with agricultural life and processes. I grant that a sceptical reader might argue that his descriptions of sheep-raising in *Far from the Madding Crowd* are as 'got up for the occasion' as the rhetorical elevation of Eustacia; indeed, the survival of an early draft of one trial scene indicates that in the flurry of composition Hardy knew so little about the process that he could only sketch it out in the broadest terms, to be filled in later, presumably by querying farmers or by going to observe and take notes on the operation. But there is a considerable difference between Hardy's larding a passage with evocative, aggrandising allusions from a body of knowledge not inherently related to the

scene to which it is being applied, and his addition of details
and clarifying relationships amidst a process which exists
nowhere *but* in the social class and time in which the particular
novel is set. In the case of such passages as 'The Queen of
Night' Hardy imports materials he hopes will allow the scene
to achieve an impact equivalent to the impact of the original
works and myths from which the allusions are taken; for
scenes of rural life he adds such details that accurately and
fully convey the essential ethical point that in the agricultural
milieu practical skill and observation of details give their
possessor – here, the novelist – inherent merit. By the time
of *Tess*, Hardy's skill with both classical allusions and with
details of agriculture has increased, so that there are few
awkward intrusions of classical allusions and numerous successful evocations of subtle differentiations in agricultural life,
from the milking of cows to the grubbing of swede roots.

In the case of *Tess* it is difficult to separate one of its primary
background features from the other, and so I want to deal with
forces agricultural, moral, and literary, recognising that often
it is not possible to keep these concerns cleanly distinct.

Wessex

Many writers are associated with a setting or location: Scott
and the Lowlands of Scotland, Dickens and London, Trollope
and Barchester, Faulkner and Yoknapatawpha County. Scott
and Dickens present real locations in imaginative colouring.
Trollope and Faulkner create alternative locations, impre-
cisely correlated with actuality. It would be a vain if enjoyable
parlour-game to attempt to draw distinctions among these
writers and Hardy; suffice it to say, perhaps, that his imagination becomes characteristically realised in plot and characters
only in those narratives which allow and require him to con-
centrate on the physical details of a genuine locale, the county
Dorset and nearby districts of the west of England.

The scholar who has given the fullest study of the entire subject of rural literature, and has with particular care studied
Wessex, takes a somewhat different tack towards identifying

the specialness of Hardy's Wessex. W. J. Keith observes that although Hardy 'belongs unquestionably to the "realistic" tradition of regional writing, with an emphasis on accuracy and verisimilitude', there is also a strong element of the imaginative. 'Wessex is offered as a "partly real, partly dream-country".' Keith seems to be suggesting that an index of this doubleness is Hardy's continuing to assign fictitious names to carto-graphically precise locations. 'His own Wessex map contains the warning: "It is to be understood that this is an imaginative Wessex only, & that the places described under the names given are not portraits of any real places, but visionary places which may approximate to the real places more or less" ' (Keith, *Regions of the Imagination*, 92). Keith's description is accurate, but perhaps limited as an explanation for the unparalleled depth of appeal that Wessex makes.

It is difficult to reconstruct the truth of a life of imagina-tion, because from our perspective we are able to see it only as a completed act. Some awareness of Hardy's way of con-ceiving Wessex can be gained by an acquaintance with the Wessex novels as he revised them several times, with the con-cept of Wessex increasingly forming one of the factors in revision. But did Hardy in 1870 have an imaginative approxi-mation of Wessex in mind as he wrote *Desperate Remedies*, or in 1874 as he wrote *Far from the Madding Crowd*, in which the word itself first appears? The truth appears to be that in his early career he was trying out a number of approaches, and that it was only through trial and error that he produced such work as the London-based *The Hand of Ethelberta* and the comparatively rich scenic background of the otherwise abstract *Two on a Tower*. This caused Hardy to realise that both aesthetic and economic gold lay in his ability to draw out evocatively the relationships between the personalities in his imagination and his profound sympathies with the physical sur-roundings amidst which he had grown up, and to which he returned, after years in London and in various basically rural spots. After only a few of his Dorset-based stories were in print, the area in which they were set became tourists' Meccas, a phenomenon of which he was keenly aware (see Keith, 'Thomas

Hardy and the Literary Pilgrims' 80–92, and Hardy's comment '*Apropos* of all these books on Dorset, & Wessex', *Letters* III. 216 (4 July 1906)); and he realised he might profit from this by producing an 'Annotated edition' with guide-book notes for new editions of his novels (*Letters* III. 16 (31 March 1902)). Such an edition was never produced by Hardy, but he had already earlier extensively re-adjusted locations, directions, and distances in the revisions for the 1895–6 Osgood, McIlvaine 'Wessex Novels' edition, and his concern for accuracy and shadings of the sites of his stories caused many of the revisions he made later for the 1912 Macmillan 'Wessex Edition'.

He had made this recognition before he began *Tess*. It seems impossible to pinpoint a date, but most likely he had realised what called forth his strongest work before he began work on *The Mayor of Casterbridge* in 1884. He had decided to build a house near Dorchester, wearying of furnished lodgings and having decided he needed a permanent residence. His brother and father built it from Thomas's own design, in such a solid and stolid form as to establish himself worthily amongst the local middle-class and professional families. (Nothing he built or wrote or did suggested he held himself with the gentry or aristocracy.)

One can, however, conjecture the process by which Hardy came to imagine scenes that 'became' Wessex. If we can plausibly suggest that his unpublished first novel *The Poor Man and the Lady* and his first published novel *Desperate Remedies* were among the experiments that did not, for Hardy, work out, the first thoroughly Hardyan novel is *Under the Greenwood Tree*. One inspiration for this novel may have been the praise of Alexander Macmillan's reader, John Morley, for the strength and freshness in Hardy's portrayal of country life in parts of *The Poor Man and the Lady*. Another inspiration for Hardy's use of rustic touches may well have come from George Eliot, who in *Adam Bede* and, to a lesser extent, *Silas Marner*, drew upon both the humour and practical-mindedness of non-genteel members of the agricultural society, in a manner which Hardy dwelt upon and took further than Eliot had done, in *Far from the Madding Crowd*, which indeed, published anonymously, was by one reviewer attributed to Eliot.

Another powerful shaper of the way in which Hardy handled physical setting was R. D. Blackmore, whose *Lorna Doone* was published in 1869 and was widely read. Hardy claimed he had not read *Lorna Doone* until 1875, which may be so; in any case, the letter to Blackmore in which Hardy notes this occasion makes one realise the close similarity of one part of their talent. Hardy noted

'how astonished I was to find' that *Lorna Doone* contained 'exquisite ways of describing things which are more after my own heart than the "presentations" of any other writer I am acquainted with . . . Little phases of nature which I thought nobody had noticed but myself were continually turning up in your book — for instance, the marking of a heap of sand into little pits by the droppings from trees was a fact I should unhesitatingly have declared unknown to any other novelist till now.'

> (Sutton, *R. D. Blackmore*, 51; the quotation
> is from Hardy's *Letters*, I. 37–8)

A passage in the pre-1875 novel *Far from the Madding Crowd* of which this note of praise reminds one is the description of the small, almost unnoticeable ways of the snails and sheep in alerting Gabriel Oak to the coming storm on the eve of the harvest supper. Sutton elsewhere in his study makes interesting contrasts between Hardy and Blackmore. For instance, he suggests that Hardy's description of Blackmore Vale in chapter 2 of *Tess* is of a permanent, unchanging scene — 'The atmosphere is unchanging; the scene stays essentially static as it is laid out in a series of main clauses that assert being only. Things either are or seem; they do not appear in distinctive action' — whereas, in contrast, 'Blackmore treats change as essential' (Sutton, *R. D. Blackmore*, 127–8). Again, while observing that initially, in 1875, the two men were not far apart, Sutton notes that both Blackmore and Hardy saw rural life vanishing, 'but where Hardy's vision turned bitter and tragic, Blackmore's remained comic' (ibid., 131).

Tess contains perhaps Hardy's most ambitious conceptualisation of Wessex. Wessex is, at all events, more variable than in other novels, both in its suasive and consoling aspects and in its ominousness and potential violence. As in other Hardy novels, the concept of 'Wessex' contains both humanity and nature: Wessex is a geographical setting whose actual locations, which can be found on a map, are sited within a culture, and the forces of nature are frequently (but not always, *vide Two on a Tower*) yoked in symbiotic relationship with that culture or society. The heath in *The Return of the Native* is perhaps the prototypical instance of this identity, encompassing at once the barrows from extinct cultures, the heather and rain, and the contemporary heath-dwellers which both provide a perspective upon Egdon and affect it materially not at all. Egdon is an expression of humanity's isolation within a specific, physical world. While the setting in most of Hardy's other novels is fairly restricted in range, the action of *Tess* is spread over nearly the entirety of Dorset, the core of Wessex, from the northern part (Marlott) of Dorset to the western (Emminster, where Angel's parents live) to the north-eastern (Trantridge; The Slopes) to the south-eastern (the Valley of Great Dairies). This range is rivalled by the way *Jude the Obscure* is expanded *out* of Wessex into the Aldbrickham (Reading, Berkshire) and Christminster (Oxford) areas, as if Hardy is finding it necessary to move into the larger world; and in *Jude the Obscure* the balance between nature and culture is being lost, so that humans are forced to wander on the periphery of 'home'. There is a quality, perhaps, of this in *Tess*, in that the tensions are more intense between location and emotion, where Marlott is a consoling, if ultimately unavailing, recourse from class exploitation, where Flintcomb Ash is a near-allegorical expression of the harshness of both raw and cultivated nature.

Social conditions of Wessex and their interpretation

In 'The Dorsetshire Labourer' Hardy in 1883 had treated in reportorial, almost anthropological style the condition of farm workers in the late nineteenth century. Sometimes nearly the same words are used in *Tess* as well as echoing sentiments, as the extended generalised analysis of Hodge in 'The Dorsetshire Labourer' is condensed and given specificness in Angel's awakening to the individuality of the farm labourers around him (18: 123). Hardy wrote the novel during what turned out to be nearly the last years of a massive but complex shift in the nation's economic forces, whose effects accorded it the name 'the Great Depression'. Twentieth-century historians have argued about the extent and nature of this Depression, and about which groups of workers were the most seriously affected by changes in purchasing and manufactory patterns (e.g. S. B. Saul, *The Myth of the Great Depression*, 1969; 1979 with corrections). It has been generally felt that agriculture was especially hard hit. Corn-growing counties suffered, while counties which produced milk had a steadier economic base; but in any case the agricultural counties and the workers in them were at a low economic state in 1888–90. No county was of a less urban culture or economy than Dorset, with its milch-cows and orchards and grain fields, its near-total lack of industry. As Richard Heath put it in 1872, 'the labourer in Dorset has been, and still is . . . worse off than in any other part of the land'. The situation had not changed markedly when his essay was collected in 1893 (Heath, 'Peasant Life in Dorset', 121).

But it was not just the immediate economic condition of the area in which Hardy was living that the novel hearkens to. He recognised that an entire way of life crucial to his deepest emotional reactions had been steadily eroding since (and indeed before) his birth in 1840. There is some dispute as to the time setting of the novel: Carl Weber, in defending his theory that each of Hardy's Wessex novels covers a different time-span, thereby providing a total imaginative history of the area, places *Tess* in 1884–9; John O. Lyons uses references to Brazil emigration schemes in the novel as reason to place the novel's events in 1869–74 (Lyons, 'The Chronology of *Tess*', 23–8). But Hardy does not clearly intend a restricted temporal location; the references to specific public issues seem more adventitious and opportunistic than cues. One is reminded of the directly contradictory evidence which can place the action of *The Woodlanders* shortly after 1857, some years after the American Civil War, or after 1878. Perhaps the most helpful statement is Hardy's own, in the Preface to *Tess*, that 'the novel embodies the views of life prevalent at the end of the nineteenth century, and not those of an earlier and simpler generation' (5), granted that he may have in mind the intellectual and affective framework rather than the historical or political.

Whatever the resolution of such arguments, *Tess of the d'Urbervilles* portrays simultaneously the energy of traditional ways and the strength of the forces which are destroying them. The novel is rich in cognitive and dramatic as well as poignant imagery that conveys the nature of life in a rural district during the nineteenth century – the continuance of folk customs such as the May Dance (which is as much pagan as Christian, but no longer expresses any vital religious suggestion at all); the formulaic but unaggressive manner of operating a dairy, with loving nicknames for the animals and folk explanations for such problems as garlic taste in the butter (Dairyman Crick thinks the milk is 'bewitched' before he realises the taste is that of garlic) and failure of the butter to 'come'; hauling the dairy products across a moor to a distant railway station, where 'modern life [had] stretched out its steam feeler', and where they are taken from their 'secluded world' to be used in London by babies who had never seen a cow (30: 187–8). Grubbing for roots in a cold field, where there is no substitute for hand labour, is implicitly contrasted with the tending of a threshing machine, with its demonic operator and its voracious maws, where Tess is reduced to a servant of the machine. Part of the power of this aspect of the novel comes from its thrust toward a future that offers none of the emotional buttress that traditional ways offer. And a good deal of the poignancy of the novel, to a twentieth-century reader, arises from the recognition that the practices that in *Tess of the d'Urbervilles* are revolutionary and destructive of the calming ways of old have for us become the reassuring ways of tradition, which in their turn have become challenged and are being destroyed by further advancements in technology, to the extent that now two or three skilful workers operating complex machines, and supported by agricultural chemists and field engineers, are able to work larger plots of land and to entice vastly greater amounts of grain from the fields — thereby further reducing the rural population and increasing the number of city dwellers and the anxiety of rural dwellers at risk of unemployment. 'Progress' continues.

Also, however, the erosion projected in *Tess* is in good part only in details — in methods of harvest, in knocking down cottages where the life-lease had expired. Hardy's larger view of existence reveals that much of past-bound rural values had not changed. There is still the power of the sun to evoke mythological implications and to remind us that myths of nature underlie social conduct and expectations; there is still the tolerance of moral 'failure' that the field workers with delicacy show Tess when she suckles her baby during a break in their work; and, most significant, there are still in tradition-focused communities the harshness and bigotry and indifference of its members towards others not of their own families, as we see in the latter part of the novel, when Tess's past, now seen as scandalous and threatening to the morality of local young girls, is made one of the excuses for refusing the renewal of the lease of the Durbeyfield cottage after John's death. This last in conjunction with the second suggests the absence of coherence in traditional behaviour. The novel offers no recourse of a hazy aura of sentiment and romanticism endemic in other elegies to departing ways of life: *Tess* iterates rock-hard observations of the often debilitating work performed in an agricultural setting that makes life there possible; its lack of sentimentality in portraying skinned and abraded hands, the aching hands and acrid smoke of the March grass-burning that clears the garden allotments for planting, is founded in the author's awareness, even if learned through observation and reading more than through experience, of the effect on the work-day activities of workers like Tess of the phenomena denoted in such romantic phrases as 'the turn of the seasons'.

There has long been an interest in employing so-called 'Marxist' analysis as a means of perceiving and defining the relationships between a linguistic artifact and the society during which it was created, and, for many critics, the society during which it is being read. Early practitioners like Arnold Kettle saw the relationship as a direct one: *Tess* portrays the rural society in decline, the destruction of the working class by members of the exploiting class (Alec and, only somewhat less obviously, Angel). The supposedly ameliorative, protective, paternalistic role of owners and managers of the economy is based on fraudulent language, its actual purpose of social control carried out with as much force as necessary. Kettle eventually modified his view that the novel is a simple reflection of an economic repression, but his direct approach of analysing fiction from the standpoint of economic pressures still occurs in popular writing, particularly in that appealing to 'common readers'. In more recent years academic critics have been using more ambitious but less direct forms of Marxist analysis, which generally are more verbally demanding but less clearly distinguishing in judgement than Kettle's. But without insisting on macro-economic and -political intentions, Hardy insists on being taken seriously, that is, as a writer of discrete passages whose meanings are determined by their own utilisation, not by preordained values.

As a reader of such system makers as Auguste Comte and Charles Fourier, and a sometime admirer of Herbert Spencer, Hardy was attracted to ambitious pretensions to encompass all experience in ideas while excluding the occasional factual evidence that contradicted the general theory. His novels often contain protrusions of such schemes, such as Clym's plan to educate the heath dwellers being described as an effort to skip an essential stage in Fourier's prescription for sociological evolution, to raise the intellectual quality of life among the heath dwellers without forcing them to pass through the intermediate stage of social ambition and worldly advance (*The Return of the Native*); the assertion that Jude and Sue are fifty years ahead of their time implies an inevitable relationship between historical moment and personal opportunity. Numerous all-encompassing systems and their supporting underlying intellectual patterns can be identified in *Tess*, and have been, ranging from Miltonic Edenism to Positivism. But Hardy's random, opportunistic imagination is not to be restricted by preconceptions or by personal beliefs. His statement in the Preface to *Jude the Obscure* that he wrote 'impressions' not arguments and in the Preface to *Tess of the d'Urbervilles* that 'the contemplative [parts are] to be oftener charged with [i.e., blamed for] impressions than with convictions' and that 'a novel is an impression, not an argument' indicate he was fully aware of his own limitations — or strengths, as his resting on concretes may more accurately be thought. Although Hardy's specific subject in the Preface is the outrage expressed by readers at applying the concept 'pure' to Tess in the subtitle, his quotation from Schiller is appropriate for the Marxist context as well: 'They [narrow-minded judges] are those who seek only their own ideas in a representation, and prize that which should be as higher than what is. The cause of the dispute, therefore, lies in the very first principles, and it would be utterly impossible to come to an understanding with them' (4–5).

'Hodge' in Hardy's and in his contemporaries' work

Hardy's respect for the human being under the dismissive term 'Hodge' comes from personal knowledge — from his father's employing labourers and indeed from his mother's family, the ne'er-do-well Hands. He knew rural labourers and rural life well enough so that although other writers regularly revised 'Hodge' within the literary tradition of rural novels and nature writing, his own literary version in *Tess of the d'Urbervilles* is a critique of the revisionary perspective. Richard Heath in 1872 noted the error of people who reassure themselves that the harsh life of England's southern peasantry is not so wretched as it seems because the people who have to endure it are 'dull, coarse-minded clodhoppers'. Heath points out that

natures of the gentlest mould may be met with perhaps as frequently among 'dull clodhoppers' as among the classes above them in the social scale. . . The peculiarity in Dorset is that such natures are not so much the exception as the rule. The Dorset peasantry are gentlefolk by birth . . . [with] that native inbred refinement, that perception of beauty and fitness, which is almost, if not quite, a divine gift.

('Peasant Life in Dorset', 121)

Despite Heath's clear sympathy with the peasants as oppressed, and his sympathy with the rick-burners of the 1830s and his support of the Labour-Union organising of the Puddletown Martyrs of 1833, he does not see them as definite individuals. His terms stereotype and thus sentimentalise peasants in much the way of Hodge, if in an inverse direction, so that if Hodge is done away with, the Noble Savage somehow replaces him, still not entirely in a favourable light (ibid.).

But the pressure for an educated observer to generalise from observation of farm workers must have been strong, if unexpressed. Richard Jefferies, who wrote widely and sympathetically of life in the country, could declare, in the 'Preface' to *Hodge and His Masters*, 'In manners, mode of thought, and way of life, there is perhaps no class of the community less uniform than the agricultural. The diversities are so great as to amount to contradictions. Individuality of character is most marked, and, varying an old saw, it might be said, so many farmers so many minds' (I, v). (It is as if Angel, in learning about Hodge, had been taught directly by this page!) But in contradiction to this preface of volume I, in which he declares the lack of uniformity in rural life, in the two volumes that follow the 'Preface' Jefferies reinforces most of the stereotypes about rural life. He tends to think that unskilled labourers are lazy, resting between brief moments of mild exertion, and have it easy, unlike skilled workers, who have to keep at it. He seems to condescend towards the agricultural working class, and accepts stereotypes of animal-like males, even insisting upon coarse and greasy food, of slatternly women who keep the insides of cottages clean but who throw offal and rotting food in the ditch within yards of their cottages, of men loafing on Sundays (I, 150–4). But there is also an aspect in which some of these descriptions – such as the labourers 'brutalised' at the beerhouses (I, 174), the 'low cunning' of the manager of the low public house (I, 178) and his wife 'whose cheeks as she walks wobble with fat, whose face is ever dirty, and dresses (at home) slatternly' (I, 180) – are used by Jefferies as slurs to, in effect, elevate the status of Hodge, the sweat of whose brow is condensed into the diamonds worn by the wife of the owner of the pub (I, 182); and in general Jefferies suggests that 'Hodge' is not well treated by his English masters.

But however distanced or self-contradictory he may be, Jefferies knows a great deal about farm work, and Hardy could well have borrowed details of many of his scenes. Jefferies discusses farmer-apprentices like Angel: clearly his and Dairyman Crick's is not an unusual arrangement. As well as from observation around him, Hardy could have learned from Jefferies why Tess is not a bad match for Angel in the agricultural world. In 1872 Jefferies wrote that in Wiltshire 'Dairymaids are scarce and valuable. A dairymaid who can be trusted to take charge of a dairy will sometimes get £20 besides her board (liberal) and sundry perquisites. These often save money, marry bailiffs, and help their husbands start a farm' (quoted in Mabey, *Landscape with Figures*, 37–8). His description of farmers' wives and young daughters makes one realise why Tess as a carter's daughter is a better prospective wife for Angel than is Mercy Chant (*Hodge and His Masters*, I, 218, 233). He notes that it takes a larger farm than 200–300 acres to 'enable the mistress and the misses to play the fine lady,' as it would have done 'two generations ago. It requires work now the same as then – steady, persevering work – and, what is more important, prudence, economy, parsimony if you like' (I, 219). 'These days' most farmers' daughters shun physical work, and thus 'If they marry a tenant farmer of their own class, with but small capital, they are too often a burden financially' (I, 233).

Jefferies in describing women working on a farm (the female Hodge?) is more conciliatory than Hardy. Slicing roots with a machine is 'monotonous work of a simple character, and chiefly consisting in turning a handle' (II, 129); in the spring it is necessary to trim roots in the field before they are fed to animals, and this trimming is 'often done by a woman. She has a stool or log of wood to sit on, and arranges a couple of sacks or something of the kind, so as to form a screen and keep off the bitter winds which are then so common – colder than those of the winter proper' (II, 132), but his description is still quite accepting – his scene does not convey a sense of harshness, cold evidently being part of the labouring class's lot.

But − despite Jefferies's declaration in the 'Preface' of the lack of uniformity in rural life − he offers generalisation after generalisation about drunkenness, immorality of several families under one roof, etc. Even such descriptions as of the two ordinary field workers who build gardens and pigsties for themselves when given the chance, do not particularise the individuals: the very fact that there are *two* of them, and that Jefferies does not distinguish between them, underscores their representativeness (the unassuming, sober labourer: 'the real backbone of *our* [sic] peasantry' (II, 213)) rather than their separate specialities. Jefferies's portrayal of the final period of Hodge's existence is not unlike Heath's in its somewhat sentimental elevation of him as an inverse stereotype: 'Hodge, who, Atlas-like, supported upon his shoulders the agricultural world, comes in his old age under the dominion of his last masters at the workhouse' (II, 295). Even the activity of a clergyman, of necessity the sole representative of his faith in a given locale, is treated generically (II, 245–51). Thus Jefferies is less an artist like Hardy than the political commentator or sociologist. However, this distancing and abstracting are inevitable attributes of what is a survey study, an explanation of a new phenomenon, the political power of the farm-labourer class, a power that has arisen because of changing economic conditions and because of what appears to be the recognition of their coming right to vote. Jefferies himself puts the matter well, in discussing independent-minded people who, because of age and infirmity, have to go to the workhouse: 'In the workhouse there is of necessity a dead level of monotony − there are many persons but no individuals . . . [E.g.,] On [the tables] at dinner-time are placed a tin mug and a tin soup-plate for each person: every mug and every plate exactly alike' (II, 308–9).

Jefferies is as alert as Hardy to the economic interdependence of all the 'masters' in a rural setting: workers, farmers, landlords; the weather; the season; foreign producers; and 'the markets which are further influenced by the condition of trade

at large' (II, 265). Jefferies gives more details of how all these
various situations affect people's lives, and the interrelationships among the conditions of different groups of people:
because prices are falling, farmers want to pay lower rents;
because labourers know farmers are paying lower rents they
think the farmers can afford to pay higher wages; under the
pressures of expenditures farmers invest less, reducing income
and eventually causing reduction of the work-force, increased
emigration, etc. (II, 269, and *passim*). Hardy (perhaps natural-
ly) never traces matters beyond the immediate condition, so
that John Durbeyfield coming down in the world is more an
individual condition than one of many consequences of
economic dis – and re-orientations.

My point is this: although, in part, the truth is that Jefferies
(and others) and Hardy were simply describing the same
phenomena, it is also the case that Hardy, although a
countryman, was also partly dependent upon persons more
knowledgeable about rural economy for his insights and basic
thrusts. For example, Jefferies's 'Going Downhill' (I, 60–81)
traces in detail the stages of the movement from being a
hereditary farmer through bankruptcy to becoming a bailiff
on a former farm, with a knowledge of such things as drainage
and the effect of foreign grain suppliers upon the market, giving a plausibility to a kind of financial disaster that Hardy's
portrayal of Henchard's rapid fall through obsessive and
reckless speculation in *The Mayor of Casterbridge* simply
sensationalises.

If Jefferies is in *Hodge and His Masters* a user of stereotype
himself, he grew out of this attitude. As Richard Mabey has
noted, 'Jefferies' accomplishment was to portray it [the
countryside] in all shades with an equal vehemence and within
the compass of a single working life.' On Wiltshire labourers
in 1872, he stresses with 'disdain', in what is 'by any standards
a callous piece', the labourers' 'uncouthness, laziness, and more
than adequate wages'; but this is to be contrasted with the piece
written thirteen years later, 'One of the New Voters,' which
'recounted with meticulous detail and controlled anger a day

in the life of Roger the reaper' (Mabey, *Landscape with Figures*, 9–11). And again, the description of the heat in the harvest field in Jefferies's 1885 'One of the New Voters' (Mabey, 254–5) could have been a source of inspiration for the scene early in Hardy's novel where Tess gives suck to Sorrow.

Now, I would suggest that these Jefferies essays are important to know, not in order to prove *influence* on Hardy, but to show that the world Hardy describes reflects the genuine situation of his times, and also, and perhaps more importantly, to suggest that Hardy poetically sketches in the background that can be found in detail and practical ramifications in Jefferies.

There is, however, an essential difference between Jefferies's and Hardy's purpose: Hardy evokes the mythic aspect of the sun and companionableness; Jefferies emphasises that he is giving 'not a fancy sketch of rural poetry; this is the reaper's real existence' (Mabey, 256). Jefferies defends the reaper's conduct after work is over: he does not go home to read as the moralists might expect him to – instead, he goes to the alehouse.

The coarse labour of the mine, the quarry, the field has to be carried out by human hands. While that is so, it is useless to recommend the weary reaper to read. For a man is not a horse: the horse's day's work is over; taken to his stable he is content, his mind goes no deeper than the bottom of his manger, and so long as his nose does not feel the wood, so long as it is met by corn and hay, he will endure happily. But Roger the Reaper is not a horse. Just as his body needed food and drink, so did his mind require recreation, and that chiefly consists of conversation. (Mabey, 256–7)

Conversation is what he goes to the alehouse for, even though the conversation may not be thought much of by the readers of the essay. John Durbeyfield does not have the excuse of exhaustion; his going to Rolliver's Inn is a sign of the moral decay and social indifference that surround Tess. Jefferies compares the harvest scene as perceived by a non-working observer and by the farm worker:

To linger by it, to visit it day by day . . . is a delight to the thoughtful mind. There is so much in the wheat, there are books of meditation in it, it is dear to the heart. Behind these beautiful aspects comes the reality of human labour – hours upon hours of heat and strain;

there comes the reality of a rude life, and in the end little enough of gain. The wheat is beautiful, but human life is labour.   (Mabey, 260)

Given Hardy's obvious knowledge of Jefferies and the similarities in their outlook, one is tempted to see in Jefferies's wonderful mystical autobiography, *The Story of My Heart*, some source for the most inventive passages of *Tess*, Tess's moments of mystical experience — as announced by her in the kitchen of Talbothays, when she says she can make her soul go out of her body, and as portrayed by the narrator in describing Tess's reaction to Angel's harp-playing in the garden. Jefferies's description of his impassioned experience at the top of an isolated hill (*Story of My Heart*, 2–6) *could* have given Hardy some impetus towards the scene of Tess in the garden (19: 127–8); a major difference is that Hardy gives more detail and heightening of Tess's state of mind, whereas Jefferies once again simply states, without rendering, his sense that he was in an unusual mental state. For example, he presents in flat statements a mood presumably approximating to Hardy's/ Tess's synaesthesia: 'Through every glass blade in the thousand, thousand grasses; through the million leaves, veined and edge-cut, on bush and tree; through the song-notes and the marked feathers of the birds; through the insects' hum and the colour of the butterflies; through the soft warm air, and flecks of clouds dissolving — I used them all for prayer' (ibid., 18).

And consider this passage from Jefferies's autobiography:

I was sensitive to all things, to the earth under, and the star-hollow round about; to the least blade of grass, to the largest oak. They seemed like exterior nerves and veins for the conveyance of feeling to me [cf. the analogy here with the physical lines of force in *The Dynasts*]. Sometimes a very ecstasy of exquisite enjoyment of the entire visible universe filled me. I was aware that in reality the feeling and the thought were in me, and not in the earth or sun; yet I was more conscious of it when in company with these.   (ibid., 141–2)

It seems to me that Hardy's, and Tess's, sensitivity to the physical world is implicit in this passage, but Jefferies's is far more bound to the actual physical than is Hardy's.

If one can summarise such a complex subject in such a brief treatment, it is quite possible that Hardy knew *The Story of My Heart* as well as other Jefferies writings. But Jefferies's mysticism was too cerebral and too distant from the actualities of the interactions and conflicts of personalities to have a steady and unmistakable impact on Hardy. The customary analysis of Jefferies's weakness as a novelist lacking a sense of character suggests the principal difference between his mysticism and Hardy's: by sticking with himself, Jefferies permits a gap to develop between the specific details of nature and life and his explicit abstract perorations about their significance, whereas Hardy transplants into personality (Tess's) — and is able to convey to his readers — what it meant to have such mystical, religious but not theological, profound but not judgemental responses to mundane, available moments of experience.

Chapter 3

Some literary influences

An essay on literary influences on a novel as rich as *Tess* can scarcely do more than touch on a few of the stronger or more interesting predecessors. The book crystallises the Victorian period in the way it brings into its point so much of its literary surroundings. And, of course, some things we may think of as 'influences' may be nothing more than similar responses by Hardy and other writers to similar information and attitudes.

Chastity in nineteenth–century life and writing

One of these areas is certainly that of sexual morality in life and fiction, including *Tess*. It is commonly stated that Victorians shied away from direct mention of sexual life, yet nearly every Victorian novel is founded to a greater or lesser extent exactly upon the question of 'given the man and woman, how to find a basis for their sexual relation', as Hardy defined it in the Preface to *The Woodlanders*. Novels were selected for publication in mass-circulation magazines on the criterion that they could be read in rural parsonages to young daughters — a standard which several of Hardy's novels did not meet, according to letters from the parson fathers which have survived in publishers' archives. Yet, in many of the same rural districts served by the parsons, conditions in the farm workers' two-room homes were so crowded that, as church boards declared, immorality (by which here they meant incest) was almost inevitable. More rural wives were pregnant at the time of marriage than those who were not. The attitude of Joan Durbeyfield toward Tess's going to work for the fake d'Urbervilles may be calculating and callous, but in moral terms it would not have been considered particularly slack: 'Well, . . . she ought to make her way with 'en, if she plays her trump card aright. And if he don't marry her afore he will after' (7: 55).

It is Hardy's *Jude the Obscure* that is usually discussed in relation to the New Woman novel of the late nineteenth century, but it is more the culmination of the movement. *Tess of the d'Urbervilles* was written in the midst of it, at about the same time as Sarah Grand's *The Heavenly Twins* (1890; publ. 1893), for example, and no doubt contributed towards the vitality of such novels written soon after it as Grand's *The Beth Book* (1897). Both of Grand's novels dealt with venereal disease, adultery, and unconventional marital arrangements. George Egerton's *Keynotes* (1893) expresses women's ideas on sexual experience, and the heroine of Grant Allen's *The Woman Who Did* (1895) is a woman who insists on living with a man without benefit of clergy. This is a near parallel in some respects to *Jude the Obscure*, as is Allen's *English Barbarians* (1895), which presents the argument that marriage should be dissolved on the wish of either partner. Interestingly, Allen defended *Tess of the d'Urbervilles* in his 'Fiction and Mrs. Grundy' (*Novel Review*, July 1892; *Letters* I. 277). Perhaps those who complained so vehemently about the moral indeterminateness of *Tess* recognised its power in potentially inspiring other, more directly iconoclastic novels.

It is striking, for instance, that readers still disagree vehemently over the question of whether Tess was raped, or seduced, by Alec in The Chase. There appears to be no resolution to the issue, nor to Hardy's intentions about clarifying the dilemma in several reconsiderations of the scene over the years (see Grindle and Gatrell's 'Introduction' to their edition of *Tess*): the totality of his alterations suggests he wishes to draw out the ambiguity rather than clarify the act as violence, persuasion, or co-operation. This is also the conclusion of Leon Waldoff, who has thoroughly evaluated the evidence (Waldoff, 'Psychological Determinism', 140). Ultimately, Alec's culpability seems not to be one of the novel's important cruxes. The novel is concerned less with coercion than with consequence – the consequence, that is, for Tess. The entire remainder of the novel, after her escape from the 'frying pan into the fire' on the evening of the dance in Trantridge, is a working out of the meaning of this experience — yet its precise nature cannot be determined, and it would not matter, for the world in which Tess lives, what its precise nature was. The fact that Hardy's entire narrative method underscores is the inessentiality of the fact, both because the 'fact' cannot be known apart from context, and because the society which judges Tess and helps shape her own self–judgement does not distinguish, in effective terms, between submission and passion, between ineffective will and lack of will. It is Angel's reaction that matters to Tess, and for Angel it is the continued physical existence of the man that he cannot get out of his mind; it is precisely on these narrow grounds that Tess finds the justification to take revenge for whatever was the act perpetrated upon her, or which she co–operated in, in The Slopes. As in so many situations in reading *Tess of the d'Urbervilles*, in the matter of rape/seduction relativity is all, and nothing.

The portrayal of sexuality and chastity in *Tess* makes it difficult to think that Hardy was not remembering Elizabeth Gaskell's *Ruth* (1853) while planning the history of Tess and Alec, particularly concerning their situation in their second meeting. Chapter 24 of *Ruth* ('The Meeting on the Sands') has many details which appear, usually somewhat modified, in *Tess of the d'Urbervilles*: Ruth's seducer (originally called Mr Bellingham, but now Mr Donne, having 'changed his name for some property', giving an interesting parallel with Alec, who is a Stokes pretending to be a d'Urberville). Having discovered that he and Ruth had had a son, and wanting again to be her lover, Mr Donne threatens to reveal their history, but when she refuses he offers to marry her. This is the inverse of Alec's situation, in so far as when he and Tess meet again he has recently been converted to Christianity and his first offer to her is marriage; it is only when this avenue is closed to him that Alec abandons Christianity and begins to pursue her. A further parallel with Tess is that Mr Donne promises to do good things for Ruth's family, including educate his son and settle a sum of money on him.

In chapter 25 ('Jemima Makes a Discovery'), Jemima

Bradshaw deduces from a chance remark by her milliner that Mrs Ruth Denbigh was the Ruth Hilton who had been living in sin. This ends her jealousy of Mrs Denbigh because her own former suitor has come to love Ruth, partly because Ruth had clearly been bothered when she realised that Mr Farquhar had fallen in love with her, but mostly because Jemima knows that Mr Farquhar would never marry a woman with a scandalous history. Jemima, like Tess, considers the possibility of restoring sexual purity: 'It might be — she used to think such things possible, before sorrow had embittered her — that Ruth had worked her way through the deep purgatory of repentance up to something like purity again; God only knew!', and, like the milkmaids in *Tess*, Jemima, although a 'competitor' for a man's love, is not deluded into thinking that Ruth is not an exemplary person: 'And yet, if — there was such woeful uncertainty and deceit somewhere — if Ruth— No! that, Jemima with noble candour admitted, was impossible. Whatever Ruth had been, she was good, and to be respected as such, now.'

In the next chapter Ruth says, when Mr Bradshaw refers to Ruth's son Leonard as a 'bastard', 'I cannot bear it — I cannot bear it!' This may be recalled in Tess's 'Don't make my punishment more than I can bear', but Hardy's phrase has tragic resonance, while Gaskell's is essentially only emotional. One could say that the expression in Gaskell's novel is more poignant, whereas Hardy's is intended to make a connection with a generic situation. This is a point generally valid concerning *Tess*: the novel is not 'realistic' so much as a complicated literary creation, as is evident from its allusions to tragedy, its mysticism, its evocations of mythic significance of the sun. That *Tess* has had a longer 'life' and offers more opportunities for different interpretations than Gaskell's novel suggests that modern critical theory may have a point in attributing the longevity of reader interest in a literary artifact less to its portrayal of 'truth' than to its self-reflexiveness and literary connectiveness, because, apart from occasional stereotyped Christian reactions such as looking to heaven, *Ruth* more plausibly presents life's problems than *Tess* with its melodramatic intensity and extremism.

It is probably fair to say that *Tess* is the story that *Ruth* might have been had Leonard died, just as — to look at a novel which is a direct response to *Tess* itself — George Moore's *Esther Waters* is the story of Tess had Sorrow lived. I discuss *Esther Waters* below in 'The Influence of *Tess*' (chapter 7).

It is of course a fairly direct matter to note parallels in plot and characterisation and social standards in two novels so obviously dealing with the same basic issues as *Ruth* and *Tess*; and possibly it is similarly reasonable to think that Hardy in constructing Tess's character must have had in mind Lucy, the heroine of George Meredith's early novel *The Ordeal of Richard Feverel* — they have the same innocence initially and permanently (although Lucy has more practicality), and the early courtship scene anticipates much of Hardy's garden scene in which Tess hears Angel playing his harp. It is possible to locate other fairly specific possible influences on the moral dilemmas presented in the novel. Angel's early history, and his confession to Tess, take their place in a recently developing Victorian motif. The novel's manuscript contains evidence that Angel's confession initially concerned religious doubts and perhaps even atheism, while in the published version the confession deals with sexual dalliance. William Hale White's *The Autobiography of Mark Rutherford* (1881) and Mrs Humphrey Ward's *Robert Elsmere* (1888) are probably the original 'inspirations' for the story of Angel. White's parents were religious, but he had lost his faith and turned from the Church to work for the betterment of society, a somewhat more idealistic course than Angel's, but with a not dissimilar spirit of earnestness. The hero of *Robert Elsmere* attempted to make up for a wasted youth; his spiritual struggles allowed him to serve as a model for a generation of young people in the 1880s. When Hardy decided to make Angel's guilt stem from un-chastity — thus heightening the hypocrisy of the Victorian double-standard — he may have taken some suggestions from George Moore's *Confessions of a Young Man* (1888).

Similarly, fairly minor points about direct influences are that some of W. H. Hudson's stories about South America could have affected Hardy's choice of Brazil as the place of Angel's pioneering venture; and Olive Schreiner's *The Story of an African Farm* (1883) could have been an indirect model for the anti-traditional ideas concerning the sexes that Angel picked up in Brazil.

General literary effect on Hardy

Both in my discussion of the agricultural environment of *Tess* and in my sketching some of the background of the novel's portrayal of sexuality, I have looked with a fair degree of confidence for antecedents that Hardy would have been aware of. More problematic is the attempt to assert connections with writers whose impact on Hardy amounted to the absorption of attitude and technique. Here I want to suggest only one general influence, Emile Zola, and one thinker whose bearing upon Hardy's manner of writing has yet to be fully explored, Walter Pater. Zola's *Nana* (1885) clearly has resemblances to *Tess of the d'Urbervilles*, although it was not necessarily an 'influence'; by the time of *Jude the Obscure* Zola's example was providing Hardy more with a tone and pattern than he found useful for *Tess*. That Zola's English publisher, Vizetelly, was twice convicted and once imprisoned in the late 1890s would certainly have made Hardy aware of the risks of this model.

Perhaps the most pervasive general influence on *Tess* from a literary contemporary was that of Walter Pater, the literary critic who had been punctiliously isolating and defining his impressions in the essays that were collected in *Studies in the History of the Renaissance* (1873) and *Appreciations* (1889), and who chronicled states of consciousness and mental receptivity in *Marius the Epicurean* (1885). Along with Richard Jefferies, Pater strongly shapes the nature of the writing in *Tess*: Hardy in effect poeticises Jefferies's specificity, while, paradoxically, he draws on Pater's pointillism to reproduce the specific context of an experience. These two qualities coalesce in the famous description of Tess walking across a disused portion of the garden in order to hear better Angel's harp:

The outskirt of the garden in which Tess found herself had been left uncultivated for some years, and was now damp and rank with juicy grass which sent up mists of pollen at a touch, and with tall bloom-ing weeds emitting offensive smells — weeds whose red and yellow and purple hues formed a polychrome as dazzling as that of cultivated flowers. She went stealthily as a cat through this profusion of growth, gathering cuckoo-spittle on her skirts, cracking snails that were under-foot, staining her hands with thistle-milk and slug-slime, and rubbing off upon her naked arms sticky blights which, though snow-white on the appletree-trunks, made madder stains on her skin; thus she drew quite near to Clare, still unobserved of him.

  Tess was conscious of neither time nor space. The exaltation which she had described as being producible at will by gazing at a star, came now without any determination of hers; she undulated upon the thin notes of the second-hand harp, and their harmonies passed like breezes through her, bringing tears into her eyes. The floating pollen seemed to be his notes made visible, and the dampness of the garden the weep-ing of the garden's sensibility. Though near nightfall, the rank-smelling weed-flowers glowed as if they would not close, for intentness, and the waves of colour mixed with the waves of sound.   (19:127–8)

Hardy had met Pater in 1886. In Walter Pater, Hardy found not only a kindred spirit, but a literary and scientific theorist who could place in a general perspective Hardy's felt convic-tion that the time for dogmatism and certitude was past. Pater had succeeded Matthew Arnold as the most influential literary critic in England. In a direct line of descent and influence from Wordsworth, Thomas Carlyle, and John Ruskin, Pater attend-ed the Oxford of John Newman, who had been a strong force in the thinking of Matthew Arnold, and Pater himself later tutored Gerard Manley Hopkins. Pater had abandoned high Victorian sententiousness and encompassing generalisations, claiming with confidence similar to that of the Victorian sages who had preceded him, but with an inverse emphasis, that one's only support was in individual values and the self. For Pater, only the impressions of perception, which themselves were tran-sient and unreliable, formed the sustenance of one's life. The bearing of Pater's 'philosophy' upon Hardy's own declarations is to be seen in the Preface to *Tess of the d'Urbervilles* that 'a novel is an impression, not an argument', and in the Preface to *Jude the Obscure* that his novels are 'simply an endeavour to give shape and coherence to a series of seemings, or personal impressions, the question of their consistency or their discordance, of their permanence or their transitoriness, being regarded as not of the first moment'.

The 'seemings' of the garden are impressions — sharp and evocative but with undefinable significance beyond their communication of the intensity of Tess's feeling. The romanticism in the simile of the pollen and the pathetic fallacy in the simile of the damp garden project Tess's state of mind. She identifies intimately with her sensuous knowledge, and she genuinely 'becomes' the totality of her experiences of sense, in a way reminiscent of Pater's word-painting of Leonardo da Vinci's 'La Gioconda' (the Mona Lisa painting), not least in the passage's suggestions of stealth and violence surrounding Tess that enrich it beyond a mere evocation of beauty in nature. Tess is at home in the garden. The smells do not offend her, nor are the garden's contents hostile to her. The passage does not prefigure her as a victim, for the verbs in the last sentence of the first paragraph in the quotation above reveal that she plays an active, not passive, part. In all, the 'message', expressed in David Lodge's words, is 'that the force of this connection between Tess and the natural world is to suggest the "mad" passionate, non-ethical quality of her sensibility' (Lodge, 'Tess, Nature, and the Voices of Hardy', 185). In this passage, Hardy's style and ideas come together in an unforgettable beauty beyond the obvious.

Chapter 4

The shaping of character in *Tess* *of the d'Urbervilles*

The characteristic of the principal actors in *Tess* that enables even the more melodramatic of them to remain viable is that they are not what they seem, and yet ultimately they *are* what they seem. By this I simply mean that, for example, thinking of Alec only as a vicious seducer overlooks his kindness and good humour and willingness to make amends; but to attempt to take these good qualities as alleviations of his essential impact on the life of Tess would be a still more serious distortion. Thus, for even the most sensitive readers, Alec is the 'wrong man' in Tess's life that the narrator indicates he is (5: 46), long before the seduction/rape; and his good qualities are essentially beside the point, although they give his portraiture the substance that makes his treatment of Tess and her murder of him a matter of regret for his sake as well as for hers. A less obvious example concerns Tess's sensual life. On her initial introduction to Alec she is portrayed as having 'a luxuriance of aspect, a fulness of growth, which made her appear more of a woman than she really was. She had inherited the feature from her mother without the quality it denoted' (5: 45). Hardy in his Victorian mode here refrains from identifying either the nature of the 'aspect' or the 'quality' the aspect denotes, but it pretty obviously refers to one's expectations of sexual interest based on possession of sexual attributes — or, to avoid paralleling Victorian coyness, it is probably safe to say that it was Tess's breasts that suggested to Alec advanced sexual maturity (see his reference to her as a 'crumby' girl (5: 46) — i.e., comely, buxom, plump). What is interesting here is that although the narrator denies that the sixteen-year-old Tess does in fact have an interest in sex, she is described within only a few weeks to have had toward Alec a 'confused surrender' and 'weakness' caused by his dazzlement of her (12: 83, 87). Again, reticence and artistic skill encourage Hardy to avoid more specific identification of female sexual desire, but his intention seems evident enough.

Tess

The characterisation of Tess offers challenges and opportunities for explication. She is described in several spots as a 'real' human being, one whose unique voice was never forgotten by those who had heard it. She is also very clearly a creation intended to be the centre of abstract and intellectual suggestions that present 'nature' in opposition to 'culture'. Indeed, it is perhaps this distinctly human indeterminateness that lies behind the narrator's iteration that Tess is a 'real' person, for example in noting 'the stopt–diapason note which her voice acquired when her heart was in her speech, and which will never be forgotten by those who knew her' (14: 99). Millgate identifies the woman as Agatha Thorneycroft (*Career as a Novelist*).

Tess seems to absorb the way of looking at life of the man in her life. She is receptive to change and impressions (16: 109); but the shifts in the tactics of her perceptions suggest something more than naïvety. Perhaps this is another indication of that aspect of the popularity of the novel which reflects wish–fulfilment and male fantasy. She surrenders – if only temporarily – to Alec's sexual energies; and at the end her revenge on Alec is parallel to Alec's second relentless pursuit of her body. In Angel's presence she veers towards mysticism – she gains his attention by describing how she can make her soul leave her body, and she loses sense of time and space in the garden scene – whereas just before going to Talbothays it had been 'the pulse of hopeful life' and 'passionate' reaction to the 'stir of generation' of the season (15: 103) that impelled Tess to go (and cf. 24: 153: Tess yields to Angel's embraces with 'unreflecting inevitableness'). She accepts Angel's gloominess about 'the hobble of being alive', 'now that you put it that way' (19: 128). When Alec tells her explicitly that she rejects whatever her husband rejects, Tess agrees 'with a triumphant simplicitly of faith in Angel Clare' (46: 311).

Tess's tragic flaw may be her d'Urberville 'reckless acquiescence in chance' (37: 248). She does not attempt any of the appeals (sexual; distress; pleading) that the narrator suggests would have succeeded with Angel. Thus, in her pride she dooms herself to having to persevere against the rigours of nature and the temptations that Alec poses. Tess's pride may be a form of self-contempt and guilt, of a type first seen in her going to Trantridge after Prince is killed.

On 4 December 1890 Hardy noted (*Life and Work*, 241), 'I am more than ever convinced that persons are successively various persons, according as each special strand in their characters is brought uppermost by circumstances.' By this time he had completed or all but completed *Tess*, although it was not to begin its appearance as a serial for another half-year. His comment defines the presentation of personality in his greatest novel. Apart from the relatively fixed positions of John and Joan Durbeyfield, characters in *Tess* are flexuous and responsive. While they project representative values in a traditional manner (Tess as a 'pure woman', and Angel as a product of the last twenty-five years), in the course of events in their lives they slither and yaw, they go back and forth, taking an action and nullifying it with an opposing action – in short, they act like normally inconsistent human beings rather than instruments of narratorial determinism. In no other novel by Hardy are the qualities of characters so difficult to circumscribe.

Hardy owes much of his standing as a novelist to the characters he created. Each novel contains at least one, and usually several, memorable portraits, characters whose interaction form the plot in good traditional and Victorian fashion. These plots developed both from the necessities of the types and from the specific qualities of the representatives of the types. To refer only to his first popular success, in *Far from the Madding Crowd* the seducer, Troy, and the reliable standby, Gabriel, circle around or observe cogently the flirtatious and fickle but basically steady and well-meaning

Bathsheba, with the hapless girl of lost virtue, Fanny, and the unstable Farmer Boldwood providing complications and opportunities for emotion-revealing conflict. Concreteness and liveliness in the narrative, and chances for empathy, develop from Gabriel's specific knowledge of rural life and occupations, from variations in Troy's feelings (never dishonest, but usually shallow), and from indications of Boldwood's efforts at self-control. In this respect *Tess* is not untypical of Hardy's best work.

Yet, how markedly does Tess stand out as Hardy's greatest triumph of characterisation. She does not quite overshadow all else in the novel, in the manner that Henchard does *The Mayor of Casterbridge*, where every detail reinforces Henchard's domineering antagonism towards not only other people but the very setting and historical theme of the novel. But as I explain below, *The Mayor of Casterbridge* portrays comparatively stable concepts; *Tess*, in contrast, is Hardy's most problematic novel, stable in scarcely any aspect. Neither the narratorial voice, as demonstrated years ago by Robert Schweik and Bernard Paris, nor the values represented by characters, can make the novel's discordant energies cohere. The novel's enriching qualities do not necessarily subordinate Tess, but their complexities deny to her eventual fate that moment of understanding and roundedness that convinces us, however temporarily, that we have grasped what the protagonist's adventure has been all about.

Tess is variously an innocent maiden, a passionately sensual woman, an 'almost standard woman', a woman of unusual attributes, a descendant (for good and ill) of the d'Urbervilles, a martyr, a sharer of insights into the significance of life, a person whose insights can be unstable, someone who alternates between being almost neurotically accepting of guilt and defiantly self-defensive, between acquiescence and rebelliousness. Often these roles are simultaneous and overlapping, but none of them is maintained consistently. Growth stemming from experience is unstable. There is something willowy about Tess's character, in itself entirely human and attractive, which cannot be ignored when one thinks about the causes of, or attempts to settle on an interpretation of, her fate. Consider, for example, the conversation between her and Alec after he has 'rescued' her from the verbal attack by the other farm labourers on the way home from the Satyr-dance, just preceding the novel's greatest crux, whether the sexual encounter between Tess and Alec is more accurately termed rape or seduction:

> "Neatly done, was it not, dear Tess," he said by and by.
> "Yes!" said she. "I am sure I ought to be much obliged to you."
> "And are you?"
> She did not reply.
> "Tess, why do you always dislike my kissing you?"
> "I suppose – because I don't love you."
> "You are quite sure?"
> "I am angry with you sometimes." . . .
> "Why haven't you told me when I have made you angry?"
> "You know very well why. Because I cannot help myself here."
> "I haven't offended you often by love-making?"
> "You have sometimes."
> "How many times?"
> "You know as well as I – too many times."
> "Every time I have tried?"
> She was silent, and the horse ambled along.   (11: 73)

The conversation well illustrates Hardy's economy, showing Tess characteristically unable to present a uniform response. Note all the times she says something yet at the same time implicitly withdraws or shifts the ground of the initial statement: 'I am sure / I ought to be much obliged to you'; 'I *suppose* – because I don't love you'; 'I am angry with you *sometimes*'; 'You have [offended me] / *sometimes*'. She is silent when Alec asks whether he has offended her 'every time'; and shortly, in response to his query whether he can treat her as a lover, 'She drew a quick pettish breath of objection, writhing uneasily on her seat, looked far ahead, and murmured, "I don't know – I wish – how can I say yes or no when –".' When Alec confesses they have gone well out of the road into the Chase, she displays a mood 'between archness and real dismay', and before he goes off to ascertain just where they are Tess seems to concur in his *stealing* a 'cursory' kiss (11: 74, 75; emphasis added).

To look thus at the scene may seem to be taking part in that complacent exercise of 'blaming the victim'. But that Alec may have perceived Tess's mixed responses as covert encouragement would not, of course, excuse him if in fact he had forced her into intercourse. The point is that Tess's behaviour here is not merely thematic or symbolic, but emblematic of the impossibility of defining in a straightforward way her personality. A similar characteristic inconsistency is in her reaction when, in learning from Alec how to whistle, she 'laugh[s] distressfully' when she has to purse her mouth and 'blush[es] with vexation that she had laughed' (9: 63). Such moments present her with the self–contradiction that is at the core of her sexual behaviour: conscious of, and even attracted by, sexual tension but denying that such feelings define her conduct. Perhaps this is another reason for her greater permanent attractiveness than other such Hardy heroines as Grace Melbury and Sue, who similarly vacillate between clearly sexual and socially constrained options in relations with men. She contains the theme of nature vs culture as Grace does, but her dilemma goes well beyond this schism, and although she embodies conventionalism vs paganism, she does so in a less dramatic or strained fashion than Sue does.

Tess is less condensable into generalisation than these other two heroines – or to put it a different way, what she symbolises is more internalised, and thus gives less of an impression of forcing the other aspects of the narrative to 'fit'. This would appear to encourage a good share of the impact of the story as being psychological, in Brooks's terms (*Reading for the Plot: Design and Intention in Narrative*). The novel is at least as intellectualised as any other Hardy novel, if not more so, in its dependence upon abstract concepts of perception and reality. But its impact is primarily emotional, centred not on the desperate condition of the world it figures, as in the evidence in *Jude the Obscure* that it is better not to have been born, but on the way the reader is implicated subconsciously with Tess beyond explanatory logic.

Inherent contradiction largely patterns the novel. Tess enters the novel both as a *tabula rasa*, innocent of knowing 'what men are like', and as a nascent philosopher who knows we live on a 'blighted' star. Subsequent experiences and reflections tend more to retain both these initial polar qualities than to meld them or to show either gaining dominance over and thereby obliterating the other.

The first major shift in Tess's character — or what is presented as such — comes after she has been initiated into sex. 'She had learnt that the serpent hisses where the sweet birds sing, and her views of life had been totally changed for her by the lesson. Verily another girl than the simple one she had been at home was she who, bowed by thought, stood still here' (12: 81). How much of this conventional view of sexuality is Tess's, and how much the narrator's, is difficult to determine, for within a few pages Tess's sense of alienation from her society is explicitly countered by the narrator, who rejects it as 'a sorry and mistaken creation of Tess's fancy — a cloud of moral hobgoblins by which she was terrified without reason. It was they that were out of harmony with the actual world, not she' (13: 91); and in due course she comes to the awareness that 'Most of [her] misery had been generated by her conventional aspect, and not by her innate sensations' (14: 96).

As she appears to be moving closer to the narrator's own evaluation of experience and morality, Tess also acquires a stature that takes her beyond her earlier portrayal as a young girl scarcely distinguishable from the other girls taking part in the May walk and dance. That her cheeks are paler, her teeth more regular, her 'red lips thinner than is usual in a country–bred girl' indicates a more subdued and lady–like appearance (14: 94). It is not clear what Hardy intends in presenting her, after referring to her 'flower–like mouth and large tender eyes, neither black nor blue nor grey nor violet; rather all those shades together, and a hundred others, which could be seen if one looked into their irises — shade behind shade — tint beyond tint — around pupils that had no bottom', as 'an almost standard woman, but for the slight incautiousness of character inherited from her race' (14: 95–6). Does he mean 'standard' as 'ideal', or as a measuring mark, or simply as a generic female? Whichever, it is clear that the point of transition is this passage, because after announcing her as 'an almost standard woman' Hardy begins to reveal her in unusual contexts, doing unusual things, such as baptising Sorrow and becoming apotheosised in the eyes of those who behold her. In determining to baptise her dying baby 'her high enthusiasm [has] a transfiguring effect upon the face which had been her undoing, showing it as a thing of immaculate beauty, with a touch of dignity which was almost regal', and in the eyes of her siblings she no longer looks 'like Sissy', 'but as a being large, towering, and awful, a divine personage with whom they had nothing in common' (14: 99, 100). Part of her appearance in the children's eyes is a matter of their perspective, of course, but the focusing action of the narrative ensures that the impact of this impression is not lost, by shortly emphasising a culmination in Tess's mental growth. Several months pass in Tess's life, but only a very few pages in the narration, after Sorrow's death, when Tess, in noting several anniversaries in her life, recognises she does not know one of the most remarkable dates of all, 'that of her own death'. She realises that when her acquaintances will say ' "It is the − th, the day that poor Tess Durbeyfield died" . . . there would be nothing singular to their minds in the statement':

Almost at a leap Tess thus changed from simple girl to complex woman. Symbols of reflectiveness passed into her face, and a note of tragedy at times into her voice. Her eyes grew larger and more eloquent. She became what would have been called a fine creature; her aspect was fair and arresting; her soul that of a woman whom the turbulent experiences of the last year or two had quite failed to demoralize. But for the world's opinion those experiences would have been simply a liberal education.

                                                                    (15: 102–3)

In most fiction such a passage would signify culmination of the narrative, possibly the end of the narration itself. In *Tess* it marks the completion of a phase − Phase the Second of the novel, and one phase of Tess's growth − but it is only interim. Not only does Tess 'fall back' from this stage of awareness or knowledge, but she repeats, more than once, the progress from hopefulness and effort towards happiness to a similar realisation. And while in one sense her knowledge deepens with each new realisation, in another and truer sense the repetition is not cumulative, but only repetitive. This, it seems, is Hardy's interpretation of life and the ultimate effect of what one learns through experiencing life − human existence amounts to a chain of attempts to gain happiness, which ends only in death. What gains such a chain the poignance so characteristic of Hardy is not only the death of the protagonist, but also the realisation of the inevitability of the repetition as long as life remains. As we will see when we consider the novel as a tragedy, Tess 'cuts off', as it were, this chain of repetition in her knowledge that for her to gain happiness a certain set of conditions must be attained and that the necessary consequence of overcoming impediments to the achievement of these conditions is her death.

But it is important to realise that in the concept of personality that Hardy is developing through Tess, even during moments of capitulative growth (e.g., 'Almost at a leap Tess thus changed from simple girl to complex woman' (15: 103)) a person retains elements of mystery and unresolvedness. Close to this passage is a description of Tess's hope that she can 'recuperate' her chastity. Hardy's precise intention concerning chastity is uncertain, but Tess is thinking of others' perception of her as a chaste person at least as much as of the physical fact of virginity. 'Was once lost always lost really true of chastity? she would ask herself. She might prove it false if she could veil bygones. The recuperative power which pervaded organic nature was surely not denied to maidenhood alone' (15: 103).

As the novel moves along, different aspects of Tess's personality are brought forward, including a deep-seated correspondence between herself and nature. As Tess leaves Marlott for Talbothays after the recuperative period, 'the stir of germination was almost audible in the buds; it moved her as it moved the wild animals, and made her passionate to go' (15: 103), and at Talbothays she describes her ability to allow her soul to leave her body (18: 125). Both of these qualities contribute to Tess's representativeness, for both are not merely her possession but qualities that interrelate her with universal forces; and both contribute largely to the novel's tragedy. But what simultaneously demands our notice is that Hardy is anxious not to make Tess solely a representative personality, or too much of one, or to elevate her consciousness beyond the realistic, despite the heroic nobility revealed in the baptism scene. The novel flares continually between the representative and the particular in Tess. In the midst of a discussion of her not having, as a milkmaid, many 'chances' in life, and immediately after complaining that she resents thinking of herself within a historical perspective in which she is 'one of a long row only' whose 'past doings have been just like thousands' and thousands', and [whose] coming life and doings 'll be like thousands' and thousands' ', her interrupting Angel at one point shows she has perhaps an equal interest in the sequence of lords and ladies in the 'lords and ladies' buds she is picking and peeling, as in the more self-conscious and melancholy and meditatively generalised topics she and Angel are pursuing (19: 130). This pattern can be detected throughout the novel; Hardy never allows Tess to exceed her humanness. That is, although her more reflective statements could be said to resemble the Platonism of Shelley, her articulation of such mental states as her mysticism is within the range of her imaginative literalness.

Indeed, Tess's simplicity and mental limitations are rather implausible in someone who, after all, is portrayed as at least somewhat exceptional in having a Sixth Standard education – although this may be primarily the residue of Hardy's early intention that she have the ambition to be a schoolteacher (see Grindle and Gatrell's 'Introduction' to their edition of Tess, 41). Hardy seems anxious to keep Tess from becoming too impressive in her cognitive grasp. Her idea of recompense for Angel's irritation at having married her is to not write to her family, to not finish a piece of sewing, and to be his slave without speaking or being spoken to (35: 227); she does not believe God would make prohibitions against adultery (12: 86); and she thinks that Angel can easily divorce her (36: 235). Her all too understandable moments of modest failing can have the largest resonances, as when, in retreating to Flintcomb-Ash from her attempt to make contact with Angel's parents and being repulsed by the behaviour of his brothers, she throws up her veil to show that she is more attractive than Mercy Chant (44: 292). If she had retained the veil, Alec d'Urberville probably would not have recognised her when she stopped momentarily to watch the preaching. Such moments of individuation ironically can enhance the counter impulse to generalisation (women as vain, their sense of self limited by their sense of their sexual attractiveness).

There is much more to be said about Tess, who after all is present either in person or by reference in nearly every scene. But considering her under other topics than personality for its own sake is necessary in order to see how Hardy manipulates her personality, and the contexts in which he reveals it. In contradiction to much of what I have said here: although one can query whether Tess progresses significantly over the first six Phases, it is certainly the case that the reader's grasp of Tess and her situation becomes more complex as the novel moves along. What I have attempted to do here is to isolate a central feature of Hardy's conception of Tess — a young woman whose simplicity is kept to the forefront, which defines her as an individual even as in other ways she seeks and gains an identity of a vastly different dimension.

But some determining features of her personality can still be alluded to here; knowledge of them affects the reading of the novel. Perhaps most relevant is the readiness with which she accepts her own guilt — in the death of the family horse, Prince, in her tragedy's initiatory event, in blaming herself for Angel's propositioning Izz Huett to go away with him to Brazil (43: 285). In the latter instance she self-chasteningly says she ought to be writing more often to him: 'I have been very wrong and neglectful in leaving everything to be done by him!' Even her reaction to overhearing Angel's brothers talk about Angel's marriage falls in with the idea of her acquiescence to chance linked to guilt: she reads the scene as her own 'condemnation' as a 'scorned thing', and feels her life is 'hopeless' (44: 291). And while scarcely a theologically aware being, she reflects the cultural conditioning of Christianity in accepting blame for being sexually attractive to Alec (45: 301).

Similarly, she does not consistently question convention. Although she has perceived the ultimate pointlessness of the struggle of life, the arguments she employs to counter Alec's new-found religiosity are not developed from her own experience but remembered from Angel's pedantic disquisitions. This has an importance beyond the thematic, as if Hardy were employing Tess for more critical issues than the refutation of theology. Following his relapse, she attempts to argue Alec out of a hedonistic position. In the words of the narrator, she knows he has 'mixed in his dull brain two matters, theology and morals, which in the primitive days of mankind had been quite distinct'; but because she is a 'vessel of emotions rather than reasons', she makes no progress (47: 320).

Angel

On Angel's first appearance he has 'an uncribbed, uncabined aspect' that suggests he has not found his groove yet, except as a 'desultory, tentative student of something and everything' (2:22). Thus, for Angel as well as Tess this is a novel of seeking or learning one's identity. He is seen initially only in outline, and in such a way that he deceives the reader as well as Tess: he appears genuinely able to participate in the rural life of club-walkings, and to accept the individual worth of rural folk. His conventionality, which comes to be realised as the dominant part of his make-up, is presented only indirectly, in the characterisations of his brothers, as if in recognition that only rarely can people escape their backgrounds. This uncertainty in Angel is something the narrator comes back to again and again, as in noting that Angel's appearance at Talbothays suggests high qualities, with no definitive aim regarding his material future, but not indecisive (18: 119). Clearly the lack of direction is central to Angel's course: he spends 'years and years in desultory studies', then goes into farming because of an acquaintance who is 'thriving' in the Colonies (18: 121).

Angel is throughout fluctuating between a rationalistic idealism and the corrective of concrete occasions. He quickly discovers that 'Hodge' is an inaccurate creation of the newspapers (18: 122); but, despite this discovery, he is 'ever in the habit of neglecting the particulars of an outward scene for the general impression' (18: 123). Hardy thus provides early, in Angel's first major appearance, an adumbration of his behaviour when confronted by the recalcitrant facts of Tess's seduction by Alec – not only on his wedding night but on his return from Brazil. Angel, in short, is not able to respond to the demands of lived experience; and in light of this characteristic, whose predominance in his make-up Hardy makes sure we realise, his accepting attitudes towards Tess during the idyll after the murder of Alec should not be sentimentalised. As Hardy himself said years later in a newspaper interview, in years to come, had Tess lived, Angel would have taunted her for her second 'sin'.

The narrator manipulates Angel's existence at frequent points to absorb it within Tess's. In this he is much like Alec and the other actors, of course, but Hardy's exploitation of Angel has more subtlety. In the earliest scene, which I discuss in detail in the section 'Adumbrations', Angel's and Tess's consciousnesses have a striking common consciousness. And when Angel appears the second time, at Talbothays, the narrator says he 'rises out of the past' (18: 119), which in the novel could refer only to Tess's past; obviously the paragraph is told more from the narrator's point of view and judgement than from Tess's (who could not, of course, know what people said about Angel when he was a lad). Angel posits himself as a kind of narrator when he asks Tess how such a young girl as she can see that 'this hobble of being alive is rather serious' (19: 128); that is, he thinks he is able to tell the anticipatory narrative of Tess (innocent and virginal), although he is revealing his inadequacy as a narrator in not being able to project himself into someone else's different course of development, to see how she might have arrived at the same point as he has.

This intensifies a central irony of the novel, that Angel is the character whose conscious, mental grasp of things most closely approaches that of the narrator (and author). This is particularly, if indirectly, stressed in passages defining the specialness of Tess. It is from Angel's perspective that we are given one of the more elaborated passages presenting Hardy's theory of tragedy. It includes the novel's primary exposition of the importance of subjective experiences: 'Many besides Angel have learnt that the magnitude of lives is not as to their external displacements, but as to their subjective experiences. The impressionable peasant leads a larger, fuller, more dramatic life than the pachydermatous king. Looking at it thus he found that life was to be seen of the same magnitude here as elsewhere' (25: 158). The use of Angel's angle of vision obviously is ironic; yet despite his pomposity, his views are not contradicted in a large way by the rest of the novel. Indeed, the narrator made much the same point after the scene in which Tess first meets Alec and after the seduction/rape.

Angel is deeply implicated in the narrator's judgements of one of the novel's most controversial scenes, the evocation of mystical implications in the music of Angel's harp and the grotesque fascination with garden slugs and images of fecundity and chaos. Given that these images dominate the scene, it is striking that Hardy chooses Angel's consciousness to evaluate Tess's self–revelations that develop from their meeting. Angel thinks Tess's untrained thoughts are like those of 'the age – the ache of modernism'; and it is from Angel's perspective that it is noted (as Hardy does elsewhere) that modern ideas are only the latest definition of ideas 'grasped vaguely' by women and men for centuries. The conjointedness of the narrator and Angel (but also their separateness) is highlighted in the paragraph, with one sentence from Angel's perspective and the next a sort of mix of Angel and the narrator ('experience is as to intensity, and not as to duration'), and the third clearly only the narrator's.

Still, it was strange that they [the 'sensations . . . grasped vaguely'] should have come to her while yet so young; more than strange; it was impressive, interesting, pathetic. Not guessing the cause, there was nothing to remind him that experience is as to intensity, and not as to duration. Tess's passing corporeal blight had been her mental harvest.
(19: 129)

At the times when Angel comes closest to the narrator's vision, Hardy places alongside him narratorial attitudes of both acquiescence and irony. Near the passage in which the psychic lives of peasants and pachydermatous kings are compared, Hardy elaborates the concept with a passage presenting simultaneously both his own and Angel's attitudes — Angel is pompous regarding Tess's humble station and person; Hardy the narrator seems at least partly responsible for the reference to an 'unsympathetic first cause', although this is consistent with Angel's educated moroseness.

> This consciousness upon which he had intruded was the single opportunity of existence ever vouchsafed to Tess by an unsympathetic first cause; her all; her every and only chance. How then should he look upon her as of less consequence than himself; as a pretty trifle to caress and grow weary of; and not deal in the greatest seriousness with the affection which he knew that he had awakened in her — so fervid and so impressionable as she was under her reserve; in order that it might not agonize and wreck her? (25: 158)

Hardy's indirect point would seem to be that had Angel been able to maintain this posture, human agency and universal energies could have been reconciled. But as already mentioned, Angel's vision is towards the general and has trouble adjusting to the specific variations that make up human existence.

The narrator judges Angel while tempering the phraseology of judgement: Angel is *too* ethereal and *imaginative*; 'Some might risk the odd paradox that with more animalism he would have been the nobler man. We do not say it. Yet Clare's love was doubtless ethereal to a fault, imaginative to impracticability' (36: 240). A point here, of course, is that although the narrator and Angel are often close, the narrator is still the judging agent in the novel, and part of his judgement of Clare depends upon his being portrayed as representative, and upon the immense destructiveness he exerts in a world of untrained impulse. The narrator explicitly says about Angel that 'this advanced and well-meaning young man, a sample product of the last five-and-twenty years, was yet the slave to custom and conventionality when surprised back into his early teachings' (39: 258). Moreover, at various points, but particularly towards the end of the novel, the narrator draws away from Angel: for example, the narrator points out that Angel still does not know life, although he thinks he does (39: 254).

For the novel to have the sort of impact he was seeking, Hardy had to allow Angel to begin to move beyond his personal anxieties and limitations and to seem to acquire larger views of issues, such as the non-essentialness of physical chastity. The question readers are forced to consider is how far he moves in this direction. Even before he leaves for Brazil, Angel begins to realise how much Tess was bound up in his thoughts of the future; and he thinks of Brazil as a place where 'the conventions would not be so operative which made life with her seem impracticable to him here' (39: 255). At this point, within days of the separation, Angel has already begun to make the *personal* adjustment to Tess's unchastity, and now the narrator stresses his concern with *social acceptance* (cf. 37: 247): 'There is that which I cannot endure at present. I will try to bring myself to endure it').

Angel realises he had supported Hellenic paganism, not Christianity, and was inconsistent in damning Tess when 'in that civilization an illegal surrender was not certain disesteem'; he should have had a similar view about his acculturated 'abhorrence of the un-intact state, which he had inherited with the creed of mysticism, as at least open to correction when the result was due to treachery' (49: 330). Or, to put it more simply, Angel revaluates Tess in a Hellenic light, where lack of chastity is not as crucial as it is in some mystical codes.

The legitimacy and permanence of the great shift in Angel's state of mind, on which rests much of the final tone of the novel, is brought into question. Angel is said to age a dozen years in Brazil; he is interested not in the beauty of life but in its pathos; and he revaluates old systems of morality to take intention, not deeds, into account, but Hardy does not show Angel's reasons for these changes. The 'true history' of 'a character . . . lay not among things done, but among things willed'. The culmination of the evolution of Angel's thinking comes when his chance, momentary companion in Brazil compares Tess's social deviation to surface irregularities on 'the whole terrestrial curve', and tells Angel he was wrong in leaving her. This man shortly dies of fever, and Angel gives his views much influence, adventitiously 'sublimed' as they are by his death (49: 328–9).

But, as is appropriate for a figure clearly supporting, rather than central to, the narrative's most powerful effects, Angel becomes almost irrelevant as an evaluating consciousness as the narrative moves towards the denouement. He is able to admit that 'it is my fault', but more telling is the fact that after Tess says she has returned to Alec ('he has won me back – to him'), Angel goes into a dream-like state and 'finds himself' in the street, walking he knows not where (55: 366). For the duration of their postponed honeymoon, Angel's consciousness as well as Tess's is marked by connotations of unreality. Wandering about, Tess and Angel are like two children whose ideas are 'temporary and unforefending', and with no plan of escape or disguise or lengthy concealment (47: 374). Tess's 'strange manner' makes Angel think she is in a 'delirium' (47: 372), and he is shown as thinking that 'the strength of her affection for himself; and . . . the *strangeness of its quality* . . . had apparently *extinguished her moral sense altogether*' (47: 372; emphases added). Angel thinks Tess's 'mind had lost its balance, and plunged her into this abyss' of 'mad grief' (47: 373). He is not certain whether to believe Tess has killed Alec or has merely attempted to do so. One would think this would be a fairly important distinction, but in order to get on with the plot as he has conceived it, Hardy allows Angel to dismiss the matter: 'It was very terrible, if true. . . . But *anyhow* here was this deserted wife of his . . .' – and he resolves to be her protector. 'Tenderness was absolutely dominant in Clare at last' (44: 373; emphasis added). Thus, in order to gloss over this striking disregard of the outcome of Tess's assault on Alec, which Angel accepts as having taken place, Hardy stresses a change in the posture of Angel toward Tess, which had been hoped for by Tess for many chapters. Angel's posture of 'absolute tenderness' allows Tess to have the period of absorption with Angel that she had been looking for, and to achieve self-identity.

There is of course irony in Angel's ignorance, and Hardy

does not altogether overlook the reader's knowledge that Alec is dead, noting wryly that there is 'no living soul between them [i.e., separating them]', and adding wittily, 'ignoring that there was a corpse' (47: 373). This presents a rather peculiar moment of ironic joshing on the narrator's part.

It is not until the men surround Tess at Stonehenge that Angel realises that 'Her story, then, was true!' (58: 381). This allows the narrative to end as if Angel earlier had been somehow granted a reasonable agnosticism on the point, which of course puts a better face legally on his escorting Tess on her flight, whereas in fact a few pages earlier (57: 373) the point had been glossed in order to prevent his curiosity, anxiety, whatever, from diverting the reader's attention from Tess.

Alec

As a fictional creation Alec is of a kind with Sergeant Troy in *Far from the Madding Crowd* and with Manston of *Desperate Remedies*. Virtues they may or may not possess are put out of readers' minds by the sexuality they exude for the female protagonists. Alec in particular, the seducer and ruination of one of the nineteenth century's most popular female characters, stands in most readers' minds as the paradigm of the mustachioed swaggerer. Hardy, in his post–publication valorisation of his heroine, made some ancillary revisions that reduced Alec still further within this paradigm (see Grindle and Gatrell's 'Introduction' to their edition of *Tess*, esp. *45–53*), but Alec also represents values which to many minds are positive.

The central fact about Alec in the novel's swirl of intellectual forces − and one commonly overlooked by readers − is that he is *not* a d'Urberville. Certainly, the novel bears, at least in part, a commentary upon the social structure of British feudalism; but Alec's role is less marked in that phase than it is in the benefit he may provide in a Darwinian manner. Alec's family, if not true d'Urbervilles, 'formed a very good stock whereon to regraft a name which sadly wanted such renovation' (5: 42). This is of course what happens, but −

presumably for reasons dependent upon another kind of symbolism (political, or perhaps psychic) – the issue, Sorrow, lacks the vitality this passage would seem to promise. Alec from the first is said to have a singular force, despite the 'touches of barbarism in his contours' (5: 43). (Matthew Arnold's barbarians were the aristocracy, ironically enough.) He is associated in this passage with rough, primeval nature in the Chase and with references to Druidism and Malthus. That Hardy did not intend him to be simply melodramatic is attested by his first speech, which combines his 'singular force' of sexuality – 'Well, my beauty . . .' – and his politeness – 'Never mind me. I am Mr d'Urberville. Have you come to see me or my mother?' (5: 43). He is clearly a character whose traits are to be shaded and manipulated for purposes of the plot and for emphases of the moment. Note, for instance, his quick 'off–stage' conversion by the Reverend Clare and his nearly equally rapid deconversion by Tess. But there is care in his presentation, for instance in the imagery employed in his early actions that implies a good deal about his character and the society of modern commerce turned 'genteel' that he at least partly represents. The strawberries Alec makes Tess eat are forced – i.e., made to ripen early (5: 44) – as Alec makes Tess 'ripen' at sixteen or so. Likewise, the roses with which he decorates her are early for the season (6: 47). Indeed, ironically, as a worker in the Stoke–d'Urberville household she herself 'crams', or 'forces', turkeys and geese in order to make them fatter than they would in nature become (15: 102).

Alec is perhaps the character hardest to fit within an evaluative scheme or psychological framework in the novel, because, even more than with Angel, our perspective on him is refracted by the use Hardy makes of him to cast some light on Tess's state of mind at different points. His chief characteristic – his sexuality – is, finally, one of the most problematic aspects of Alec. Unquestionably, he is portrayed as a Victorian rake; but the ethical implications of his behaviour are not clear in the context of naturalistic processes around which Hardy develops this novel. That he is good breeding stock for the d'Urberville line may be an ambiguous merit;

but the larger focus must be on his relationship with Tess.

The imagery of forcing conveys one interpretation of Alec's conduct toward Tess, but Hardy seems deliberately to leave open the question of Tess's exact or even identifiable feelings about Alec. She once says she never loved him, and this is never directly contradicted; but her reference to having 'been stirred to confused surrender awhile' implies some degree of willingness; and if she had not loved him, it must have been solely physical passion that subsequently kept her with him briefly. Assuming the narrator in indirect discourse reflects Tess's true mind in saying she 'had suddenly despised and disliked him, and had run away. That was all' (12: 87), the answer may be as irretrievable as the reason for Sue's abhorrence of Phillotson in *Jude the Obscure*.

This question of Tess's feeling toward Alec must be the main one for the basic operation of the reader's response to much of the novel that stems from their sexual encounter. It may not be answerable mimetically or realistically, yet without knowing how Tess feels about Alec it is hard to measure the course of Alec's feelings for Tess during her sojourn at Trantridge. To entice her to stay he promises to allow her privileges, and he evidently has given her and her family gifts; he promises generosity if she turns out to be pregnant. Her sense of the situation and her feeling for Alec, whatever it is, are what make her detest herself, and go home. It *could* be something as obvious as her sexuality – an interest in sex apart from a congenial or compatible partner – that is, a society-trained self-contempt for her own humanity ('If I had gone [to Trantridge] for love o' you, if I had ever sincerely loved you, if I loved you still, I should not so loathe and hate myself for my weakness as I do now!'). If guilt for an undifferentiated sexuality is a reasonable extrapolation from such passages, and from her 'I made up my mind [to leave] as soon as I saw – what I ought to have seen sooner' (12: 82–4), this parting scene between Tess and Alec would appear to be one of the novel's strongest condemnations of society's mores – at least as strong as that which comes after the birth of Sorrow – because such guilt restricts one's self–esteem and exercise of instinct.

What Tess's feelings may have been at the beginning of her relationship with Alec remains an open question partly because of her response to him when it is resumed. Shortly after meeting him again, she conjectures what it would be like to be able to marry Alec and get out of her unpleasant situation on the starve-acre farm at Flintcomb-Ash, in the face of 'a whole world who seemed to despise her'. In other words, she is tempted. ' "But no, no!" she said breathlessly. "I could not have married him now. He is so unpleasant to me" ' (46: 309–10). The 'now' suggests Tess is capable of feeling again the impulse of her previous temporary surrender, a possibility hinted at over and over again in her attitudes towards Alec, which intermingle both attraction and repulsion with such proleptically self-justificatory thoughts that she was 'so defenceless on account of my first error' (48: 326) and that Alec may indeed be her husband in 'a physical sense' (51: 345).

Alec's character also provides a counter-image to that of Angel. In one sense this contrast is frequently commented on by critics, as the flesh *versus* the spirit, but more significant is the essentially holistic connection Alec's religiosity makes with his sensuality. Alec's conversion amounts to a 'transfiguration' of one extreme quality of licentiousness into another extremism of religiosity: 'curves of sensuousness were now modulated to lines of devotional passion', and seductiveness to supplication; riotousness is 'evangelized' into 'pious rhetoric'. 'Animalism had become fanaticism; Paganism Paulinism; the bold rolling eye that had flashed upon her form in the old time with such mastery now beamed with the rude energy of a theolatry that was almost ferocious' (45: 297). This contrast shows that Hardy has the same insight/criticism of the bonds between evangelical Christianity and sexuality that Sinclair Lewis shows in *Elmer Gantry*, although Lewis tends to suggest hypocrisy while Hardy's implication is that the energies and psychic qualities drawn upon for one sphere of activity can be 'transformed' into analogous manifestations in the other, thereby linking the two seemingly antagonistic qualities metaphysically. Hardy's portrayal is less sensational but probably more insightful. The connection is wittily drawn by the statement that the 'corpses' of Alec's 'old fitful passions' have come back 'as in a resurrection' (46: 313).

None the less, it would hardly do to argue that Alec is instinctively religious. The analogy is placed in perspective by Tess noting that the preacher Alec's 'lineaments' seem to have 'been diverted from their hereditary connotation to signify impressions for which nature did not intend them' (45: 298) – i.e., that his physical visage betrays the unnaturalness of this role for him – and we are reminded of the statement in *Far from the Madding Crowd* that what 'is not natural is not good'. (We might also note that this passage poses a typical instance of Hardy's abstract formulation of an idea that needs to be translated or rephrased – here, explicitly; usually, internally by the reader – in order that the point of the observation be grasped. It is interesting that the point of view for this analysis of Alec is Tess's, but the language in its abstraction and its distancing from immediate visceral response could only be that of the narrator.)

An attempt to place Alec fairly must acknowledge that he looks upon Tess as a sexual object, although in being willing to marry her, and in being believably contrite at the worse deed he had done, his view of her is more encompassing and disinterested than the view of others. This is not to say that Hardy does not present him in this context ironically, as, for example, when he asks Tess whether it was 'morally right and proper' for her to marry someone else (46: 307); and he once again blames Tess for attracting him – (i.e., blaming the victim) – 'so the evil be upon your sweet head': 'You have been the cause of my backsliding.' Alec, like Angel and Tess herself, seems to feel a legitimacy in his priority as Tess's first sexual partner: he tells Tess that if she is 'any man's wife you are mine!' (47: 320–1). During much of Alec's effort to win Tess back, Hardy maintains a suspense as to whether his willingness to support her and her family is contingent upon her again becoming his mistress. The scales appear to be tipped when he tells her that they will be bound 'by all that's tender and strong between man and woman', and that their only bond will be one of trust: 'if you will only show confidence in me' (48: 324).

Given the balance of the characterisation of Alec through much of the novel, it is again useful to note that in Phase the Seventh only Tess stands as a significant entity. Alec appears only in report, in Tess's saying she hates him *now*, because he had 'lied' in saying that Angel would not return (55: 366), and in the information as the landlady listens at the door that after Tess's dirge-like soliloquy 'There were more and sharper words from the man' (56: 368). The implication of the latter sentence is functional, that Alec, having deceived and again seduced Tess, has abandoned his more gentle course of conduct. But this 'now' as the designation of Tess's coming to hate Alec is ironic, making Tess's expressed mood petulant as much as tragic in this critical moment, and again raising the question whether Tess's sexual feelings towards Alec have been consistently or entirely negative.

Chapter 5

Plot

According to Peter Brooks, plot amounts to the 'design and intention of narrative, what shapes a story and gives it a certain direction or intent of meaning . . . the logic or perhaps the syntax of a certain kind of discourse, one that develops its propositions only through temporal sequence and progression' (Brooks, *Reading for the Plot: Design and Intention in Narrative*, xi). Plotting amounts to 'that which moves us forward as readers of the narrative text, that which makes us . . . [seek] through the narrative text as it unfurls before us a precipitation of shape and meaning' (ibid., 35), portraying and embodying the 'internal energies and tensions, compulsions, resistances, and desires' in order to 'shape the creation of meaning within time' (ibid., xiv).

Brooks's is basically a conservative theory. Like Aristotle in explaining the affective power of tragedy, Brooks believes that people read in good part because of the way the plot fulfils the central functions mentioned in the last sentence of the paragraph above. Brooks is speaking not about Hardy's narratives but about the nature of narrative; but much about *Tess* becomes clearer if we look at it in the light of this strong recent analysis of plotting.

Arnold Bennett thought that Hardy's novels were masterworks of plot and symbolism. It is likely he had in mind their neat outlines, what other readers have called their architectural qualities; and one is not inclined to argue against such a concept. But in *Tess* Hardy also produced a master plot in more modern terms, in which the plot not only holds the reader's interest but conveys much of the meaning of the novel.

Many critics have attempted to explain the primacy of plot in the effect of literature. Plot helps define *myth* as well as carrying the impact of *tragedy* (according to Aristotle); and, as

the quotations above indicate, Peter Brooks thinks that it embodies the essential energies and motivations of the novel itself.
That is, the *desire* that shapes the plot (that 'which moves the
readers forward' (Brooks, *Reading for the Plot*, 35)). Brooks's
and other theorists' discussions of desire initially focus on such
subjects as sex and seduction, but their true concern is with
the principle of narration itself: 'the need to tell as a primary
human drive' (ibid., 61).

Not only are the sources and purposes of narrative thrust
in *Tess of the d'Urbervilles* essentially parallel to this ambition, as should become evident when I discuss the progress of
the novel, but in more specific ways also much of what Brooks
says is applicable to *Tess of the d'Urbervilles*. For example,
Brooks remarks that by the nineteenth century a previously
obsessive pattern of desire, the desire to stay alive, has become
ambition:

It may in fact be a defining characteristic of the modern novel (as
of bourgeois society) that it takes aspiration, getting ahead, seriously, rather than simply as the object of satire (which was the case
in much earlier, more aristocratically determined literature), and thus
it makes ambition the vehicle and emblem of Eros, that which totalizes
the world as possession and progress.   (ibid., 39)

This clearly applies to the energies vitalised into ineffectual
action by Mrs Durbeyfield, and relates both to Alec's family's
social climbing (presumably not taken seriously by people
already on that level of society) and to Angel's rejection of his
family's class ambitions (either spiritual, clerical, or academic)
for the sake of ethical fulfilment at the cost of deliberately
lowering himself socially. Angel's course suggests Hardy is
satirising – or suggesting the limitations of – this temporal
narrative desire, but Angel's ambivalent emphasis on family
also underscores the pervasiveness of the theme of ambition.
Tess does not share in her family's ambitions other than
briefly and fitfully (and later as it applies to her suitableness
for Angel); indeed, this seems part of the *tabula rasa* aspect
of her personality. She is a parody or commentary on the
modern bourgeois novel, as Brooks acknowledges (not referring to *Tess*). Brooks notes that the paradigm 'obviously

concerns male plots of ambition' and notes that a female plot is different:

The *female plot* is not unrelated, but it takes a more complex stance toward ambition, the formation of an inner drive toward *the assertion of selfhood in resistance to the overt and violating male plots* of ambition, a counter-dynamic which, from the prototype *Clarissa* on to *Jane Eyre* and *To the Lighthouse*, is only superficially passive, and in fact [is] *a reinterpretation of the vectors of plot*.

(ibid., 39; emphases added)

This sketch suggests the subversiveness of plot, which can contain both a near–deterministic pattern and an enriching divisiveness – i.e., a contradiction built upon the chosen explanatory terms. A pattern of contradiction traces the progress of Tess within *Tess*: clearly she *is* steadily seeking, and moving towards, selfhood. In her earliest act, in taking the baskets to market, she accepts herself as guilty, which in effect she later rejects, in killing Alec. She accepts herself as the salvation or hope of her family, but again later abjures this role when she kills Alec, leaving her family without support, in search of a few moments of self-realisation with Angel. Her search continues through the later repeated moments of self-torturings and musings, in the harvest fields and under the pheasants' boughs, about the degree and kind of her guilt. Her search for selfhood finds self-conscious material expression both early (going to Talbothays in almost conscious identification of herself as reflecting non-cognitive natural processes) and late (in her letter to Angel and in her killing Alec). The later events lead to the ending of the novel in a way which provides both the destruction and the meaning of the desire(s) which is/are implicit in the novel's opening scenes (as defined by Brooks, ibid., 58).

Traditional linear plots such as that of *Tess* allow for a self-monitoring that denies or complicates the expected forward momentum. The narrative drive of *Tess* bears an internal conflict. It 'expresses' secret motives: sex, ambition, self-awareness, and ultimately death. If we grant that *Tess* begins with a 'male plot' involving ambition that is deconstructed by the 'female plot' involving selfhood, there may be an underlying and inclusive plot. Brooks discusses *Le Rouge et le noir*, and suggests for that novel an underlying plot of 'strife of legitimacy and usurpation' (ibid., 69). This would not be a bad way to describe *Tess of the d'Urbervilles*. In the course of her actions and irresistible desires Tess demonstrates her own legitimacy as a d'Urberville. Her achievement of selfhood is ironic in this sense: in achieving selfhood – or in taking actions whose purpose is to allow her to achieve selfhood – she is 'selfish', just like her d'Urberville ancestors who, as they returned from a battle, had raped young maidens. She brings down the usurper; but historical-legal conditions have not changed as she has, and the authorities that legitimated illegitimacy (Stokes→d'Urbervilles) remain in power, and exact 'justice' in a fashion that the original d'Urbervilles had not had to worry about. But they lost their power and wealth during centuries of the rise of mercantilism and capitalism, and so Tess's death simply, although ironically, cements her identity as a true d'Urberville.

Other of Brooks's comments about plot throw up suggestive ideas pertinent to *Tess*. Brooks talks about the onward rush of events in *Le Rouge et le noir*. The protagonist plans ahead, does not look back: the desire is prospective, unlike in, say, Flaubert (*L'Education sentimentale*) where it looks to the past (Brooks, 77). Tess's selfhood is always in the future, but, while this is her goal, she wishes to return to the past, to her state of lost virginity, the time of the May Dance, and have Angel choose to dance with her. She wants Angel to come back so they can resume the life they never had, but which is also a thing of the past owing to Angel's nature and Tess's 'un-intact' state. Angel, while positing himself as a forward-looking man not interested in staid clerical life, and as a man willing to lower himself socially because that is where his future is, wants a wife from the dream-world of rural purity that must derive from Carlyle's ideas of past political wisdom. In *Tess of the d'Urbervilles*, as in *Jude the Obscure*, where the urge to the future is strong, when the protagonists actually begin to move to the future they are caught up short by the present as it exacts the moral standards of the past.

But one of the most basic aspects of plot that Brooks takes

up concerns the impetus to keep reading once one begins. He argues that the opening paragraph of most novels portrays a desire, a desire which each chapter keeps alive. In *Tess*, this desire may explain the effectiveness of Hardy's use of the technique of adumbration to guide readers indirectly along the complex unravelling of motive and responsibility, to enhance emotional coherence in a plot whose narrator seems to be insisting on the centrality of outside forces. 'Adumbrations' is similar in general or casual meaning to 'hints', and is near 'foreshadowings', but both these terms impart a greater degree of imposed pattern than Hardy's practice justifies. The point is that there are certain inherent qualities of Tess's character whose eventual flowering is implicit in their earliest, seemingly inconsequential forms. The significance of the earlier forms lies in the manner in which they help define action brought about by later choices. Thus one thing I want to do here is to study the opening section of *Tess* and expound on the narrative desire it represents. I will then consider how adumbration is effective in other passages of *Tess*.

Adumbrations

Many passages in the early pages of *Tess* are compressions of later developments. The effect is not so much to move the readers forward or to satisfy expectations once the later developments are reached, as it is to reinforce an impression of cohesion, and, even more, to illustrate indirectly a principle central to Hardy's work, that fate is not just an external force, independent of fiction's sequence of decision and consequence. This impression is crucial to the novel's impact because this novel is unusually rich in complexities and ambiguities, which frequently threaten the narrative with incoherence, even as they account for at least part of its mystery and appeal. An instance of this incoherence: Hardy never reconciles Tess's ordinariness and her specialness; her simple-minded literalness and her sensitivity to the explicitly non-literal; her sexual 'purity' and innocence and her sensuality and flirtatiousness – all contradictions which of course enhance her lifelikeness.

From Tess's and Angel's first meeting at the May Dance, the narrator's choice of terms and phrases registers their extraordinary sensitivity towards each other. Because of his hurry, Angel chooses a dancing partner without attempting to discriminate among those available. Tess's eyes convey 'reproach' to Angel for not choosing her (2: 23), a feeling that may appear to be somewhat egoistic, dangling without narrative foundation at this early part of the story but ominously (for Angel) predictive of her eventual blaming him for staying so long in Brazil.

Most readers will simply 'read past' such implications, a reaction Hardy recognises but one he is not fully satisfied with. Although the bearing of these implications for Tess's characterisation can wait, the narrator is also developing a judgement against the universe, and the narrator wants the reader to reflect upon this scene. Tess's first visit to Alec a few chapters later allows Hardy his opportunity. Following Alec's forcing her to eat strawberries from his hand — an adumbration in itself, as is her eating 'in a half-pleased, half-reluctant state whatever d'Urberville offered her' (5: 44) — the narrator muses:

Had she perceived this meeting's import she might have asked why she was doomed to be seen and coveted that day by the wrong man, and not by some other man, the right and desired one in all respects — as nearly as humanity can supply the right and desired; yet to him who amongst her acquaintance might have approximated to this kind, she was but a transient impression half-forgotten.   (5: 45–6)

Soon after, the narrator refers to Tess's 'missing counterpart' waiting in 'crass obtuseness' for 'wandering independently about the earth' that leads to all the 'anxieties, disappoint-ments, shocks, catastrophes, and passing-strange destinies' — a remark that may seem unfair to Angel, but which suggests that Tess was justified at the May Dance in feeling reproach towards Angel for not choosing her as a partner. In a literal sense, her reaction may seem unfair, but in another it anti-cipates the judgement by the narrator that Angel was a special person in her life, and that he should have realised it, and thus acquires a degree of blame. It is *not* the point, of course, that Tess's reaction or the narrator's endorsement of it is rational or plausible – but such is the aesthetics of Hardy's centripetal narrative, from whose energies Tess cannot escape.

Moreover, the language used in the earlier scene to describe Angel's reaction to his mischance in not asking Tess to dance with him suggests that he accepts that there is a responsibility in such matters; Angel 'instinctively felt that she was hurt by his *oversight*' (2: 23; emphasis added).

Tess is an attractive character from the first; but Hardy's skill in having her personality dominate the entire novel has at least this structural characteristic, that her behaviour at the May Dance continues to resound – although in an understated way, whose impact comes only later, when the earlier behaviour is paralleled during her seduction by Alec. Although Hardy's final thought about Tess while he was completing the manuscript caused him to add the subtitle 'A Pure Woman', his conception of her character during her first appearance in the narrative is of a teenager with normal social and emotional interests. She is attracted to Angel partly from social awareness or ambitions, because he speaks 'nicely'; then, after a time without having any spirit to dance after Angel leaves, she becomes willing to dance, and even participates 'with a certain zest', paralleling the 'confused surrender' she feels 'for a while' after she becomes Alec's sex partner. The narrator notes her sexuality, however, saying she was not aware of 'what she herself was capable of in that kind' (3: 24). Tess's return home from the dancing reveals her character and adumbrates her later behaviour, indeed encapsulates the novel's iterative portrayal of her ready guilt feelings: she feels 'a chill self-reproach' at not helping her mother with the domestic duties of child care and the washing (3: 25).

The purpose of adumbrative passages is to anticipate, in small, later and more dramatic interactions. The initial suggestions about character are justified in the later event. The simple narration of the cart-ride with Alec to the Slopes, near Trantridge, for instance, imparts information about Tess's character that helps explain her later willingness to scramble onto Alec's horse to escape Car Darch and the other labourers, and that has its full amplification only near the end of the novel. Upon Alec's first clear flirtation with Tess on the cart, she looks at him like 'a wild animal', thinking of the 'lamentable purpose' for which her mother had dressed her. She is 'surprised beyond measure' by Alec's wish to kiss her, and – in what may be an unconscious self-revelation – says 'I don't mind!' while she 'panted miserably'. After the kiss she is 'flushed with shame' and rubs the kissed spot with her handkerchief – 'She had, in fact, undone the kiss, as far as such a thing was physically possible' (8: 57–8).

This passage, occurring before Tess's seduction, suggests her essential innocence ('surprised beyond measure'), the ambivalence of her sexuality ('I don't mind!'), and her guilt at a sexuality which is at once inadvertent and intense. A gesture that seems quite innocent of significance – Tess's wiping off the kiss in a non-reflective, even automatic fashion – anticipates the later suggestion that she can restore her virginity and recuperate in nature's way from the damage done her in the Chase; and most significant of all, this gesture anticipates her unconscious reasoning in killing Alec: that in literally doing away with her past she can win back Angel. Thus, this passage, which presents merely the initial step in Alec's siege of Tess, conveys the core of the novel's action (especially as far as Alec is concerned!).

Far from dominating the narrative, these adumbrations appear in the midst of an essential straightforwardness. Hardy, without misleading his reader as to the gloomier prospects in store, concentrates on dialogue, humble events, and characters reacting to each other. It is, in short, a superlatively effective opening: Angel at the May dancing, for instance, is presented only in outline, and in such a way that he deceives the reader as well as Tess: he appears genuinely able to participate in the rural life of club-walkings, and to accept the individual worth of rural folk. His conventionality, which is to be so dominant a part of his make-up, is presented only indirectly, in his continuing to hasten to catch up with his brothers after he recognises he has 'acted stupidly' in not dancing with Tess, and in the characterisations of his brothers. With the extended powerful final passages of this Phase lamenting the 'coarse pattern' being traced upon 'this beautiful feminine tissue, sensitive as gossamer, and practically blank as snow as yet' (11: 77), the novel's purposes are made clear and unavoidable. Presumably, Hardy hoped that by that time the reader would be hooked. It is to be noted that these comments of mine about the adumbrative aspect of *Tess of the d'Urbervilles* correlate with Mowbray Morris's perception that the novel's opening draws the reader onward, in anticipation of the inevitable seduction of the heroine. The weightier tone of tragedy is seldom present in these early pages themselves, but the relatively lighter tone ceases at the end of chapter 9. With the very opening of chapter 10, the novel invokes a reality of rural life, sexual levity and drunkenness in Trantridge and at the Slopes.

The novel has many more direct hints and foreshadowings, such as Joan asking, on Tess's return from Trantridge, why she had not thought of 'doing some good for your family instead o' thinking only of yourself?' (12: 87) – which of course anticipates Tess's justification for returning to Alec much later in the novel. A reference to Tess's possession of a 'mute obedience characteristic of impassioned natures at times' (30: 188) anticipates her passive acceptance of Angel's abandonment, and her subjection to Alec before her bloody breaking loose of him at the novel's end. Most of these references are minor; I want to discuss at greater length the significance of the episode with the dying pheasants, which occurs as Tess is on her way to Flintcomb-Ash. The incident and Hardy's presentation of it are in a sense introductory to this stage of her life, in that previously she still had some money left over, and her previous agricultural jobs since leaving Marlott have been only referred to, not described in detail. The passage, then, is accretive, in that it builds upon her previous condition and even evokes certain specific instances, such as her sending money she needed for herself to her parents so they would have a roof over their heads for the coming winter. What bears emphasising, though, is the way the passage also anticipates what is to come.

To be noticed is how darkly Hardy tones the scene, albeit

using Tess's indirect point of view: 'Was there another such a wretched being as she in the world?' Tess's most arduous period — the relative degree of which of course would not be known by a first-time reader — is about to begin, at Flintcomb-Ash. This passage shows Tess about as bitter as she ever gets, including after Alec re-enters her life, although by then she is more desperate and beset than during the pheasant episode. The purpose of placing the pheasant episode here, instead of, say, during her return from the abortive visit to Angel's parents, must be to prepare the reader as she/he observes Tess's tribulations at Flintcomb-Ash. Thus, Hardy is anticipating a certain reaction, and is preparing the reader (as well as Tess!) to feel that even there, with the severe field work and unsympathetic employer, Tess as an element of a life in nature is not as badly off as the pheasants, pursued and slaughtered and left callously to suffer over-night, primarily for the purpose of aristocratic sport. Indeed, someone aware of Hardy's stand against cruelty to animals could believe that the deepest feelings in this scene are engaged with the pheasants, and that Tess's is a symbolic reinforcement of *their* situation. This passage also provides an anticipatory slant on the novel's last comment on Tess, 'The President of the Immortals, in Aeschylean phrase, had ended his sport with Tess.' The disillusionment with conventional lamentations and judgements of the value of life is clearly adumbrative of that last comment: Tess, just before the pheasants' dying sounds become audible, thinks that 'All is vanity' is 'a most inadequate thought for modern days. Solomon had thought as far as that more than two thousand years ago: she herself, though not in the van of thinkers, had got much further. If all were only vanity who would mind it? All was, alas, worse than vanity — injustice, punishment, exaction, death' (41: 270).

Given the suggestion that Tess during the previous eight months has been generally unreflective, one could criticise the implausibility of her sudden reawakening into the way of thinking that in a very early scene had characterised the earth as a blighted apple, but of course then there had been little demonstration of what had led her to have this insight. But there is another consideration. This same passage also contains a redaction of an intervening moment, which after a similar period of several months following a difficult time (the death of Sorrow) had marked Tess's advance in a bound from 'simple girl to complex woman' upon thinking that one day *she* would be dead (15: 103). That advance was also a marker for 'reflectiveness' and the 'note of tragedy' in her voice. Just preceding the sounds of the dying pheasants, Tess feels the flesh of her face and thinks 'as she did so that a time would come when that bone would be bare. "I wish it were now" ' (41: 270). In other words, the pattern Hardy has set up, with this incident of the pheasants as its dramatic and defining point, is a rhythmic alternation of Tess as a passive peasant and Tess as a conduit or even interpreter of contemporary philosophy. This is consistent with the novel's 'theme' of a search for self-identity, and with its pattern of delaying the most pertinent developments of tragedy until the final Phases, where Tess rebels against the conditions of things economic, societal, and 'moral', and declares that her need for selfhood is so intense, and worthy, that she forces its achievement, if only for a brief time before death.

For the person who has read *Tess* before, this passage involving the pheasants offers some anticipatory irony. We quickly see that, however much suffering and unhappiness there is for Tess in the time just past, what comes is more difficult, in that there are less congenial surroundings, a less sympathetic employer, and more difficult work; and the support of the dairymaids who had been at Talbothays is mixed with her awareness that they know of her treatment by Angel.

The general intention of the plot

Two features of the plot of *Tess* impress themselves on our minds. The first is that it is immensely simple and straight-forward, in both conception and in the unravelling: it is a linear, step-by-step tracing of the fate of a young woman in time and space with at least the appearance of causality and develop-ment. The second is that the plot, while thus traditional in outline, bases its unique effect upon groupings of events that have a profoundly cyclic quality. That is, Tess recapitulates her previous moods and beliefs as much as she moves beyond them. The novel's adumbrations bear upon this quality. Hardy's pacing is that of poetic or dramatic method: single lines, passages, or occurrences propel the reader. One tactic is to conclude one phase of Tess's novel-long journey with a scene or statement that seems to *exceed* the necessities of its location, giving an attitude whose appropriateness is only fully realised in the next section or even later in the novel.

As I have suggested in discussing Tess's personality, the plot is organised in good part around her search for and movement towards identity. In the first Phase, Tess is presented as an ordinary girl, liable to seduction because of her spirit, curiosity, and natural sexuality. None of these qualities is stressed by Hardy. After the death of Sorrow and after her own realisation that she herself will die, Tess changes 'almost at a leap . . . from simple girl to complex woman' (15: 103). It is in keeping with the novel's base in subjectivity that Tess becomes a complex woman after realising that the day of her death has interest to no one but her. Soon after, Tess is described as 'a visionary essence of woman – a whole sex condensed into one typical form' – in Angel's eyes – and yet she is only a dairymaid in ordinary light (20: 134–5). After Tess's confession on her honeymoon, the tone is steady and heavy – all is serious and foreboding from here on. The immediate cause is Angel's taking things so seriously – any hopefulness Tess feels is squashed instantly by his intense sombreness.

Thus *Tess* begins as a novel of simple domestic difficulty whose details become generalised in significance as Tess's initial pessimistic outlook is increasingly endorsed by events, and by the narrator in direct attacks on nature's lack of sentiment and on society's harsh judgements of 'sin'. Within this pattern there are interspersed reminders of the personal projection of values – such as the world as a psychological phenomenon – that force attention upon Tess's mental state. Thus, the reader is made receptive to sombre reflectiveness. The novel's concentration on Tess's trapped existence becomes so intense and unremitting that eventually the reader insists on a release powerful enough – murder – to balance his/her pent-up anxiety about Tess. Thinking of the plot in this fashion is a simple but not illegitimate way to consider the novel's cathartic impulse, and to identify the relationship between the first six 'phases' and Phase the Seventh. The quality of Phase the Seventh as a tragedy in itself will be taken up later.

A brief notice of one scene in Phase the Fourth ('The Rally') allows us to see how Hardy incorporates his plotting into his tragic aims, and how the novel scene by scene is so engrossing. In the perspective of the entire book, Tess's and Angel's journey on the milk-cart to the railway stop may seem minor, but in transit it holds our attention. The reader does not see Tess's indecision as waffling or coy, but through its presentation participates in the deep ambivalence as to whether Angel's primary attraction is physical sexual possession (as Tess seems to feel it) or an intrinsic refinement in the unsophisticated Tess (which comes from the narrator's perspective): 'Tess knew that she must break down. Neither a religious sense of a certain moral validity in the previous union nor a conscientious wish for candour could hold out against it much longer. She loved him so passionately; and he was so godlike in her eyes; and being, though untrained, instinctively refined, her nature cried out for his tutelary guidance' (29: 183). This ambivalence – never resolved – pervades the entire Talbothays episode. For several long stretches the reader may chafe at apparent delays in the progress of the plot. The only event we are waiting for is Tess agreeing to marry Angel, so the forces antagonistic to human happiness (48–9, 90–1) can be again displayed. The result of the slow and rich development of Angel's and Tess's love is to deepen the anxieties, the dogmatisms, and the tentativenesses of Tess at the several stages of her self-development. A similar pattern of impeded plot characterises the developments later on at Flintcomb-Ash.

Much of the impact of the novel depends on what occurs during the scenes at Talbothays. Considerable attention to agricultural details, both of procedures and of economic implications (the process of getting the milk to the train for

London; different categories of milk cows on the farm); several passages developing images (as the above, in a modest way) and their metaphysical implications (especially in the garden scene, which of course is a demonstration of the keen receptivity of Tess's emotions, not crippled because of her social and intellectual standing); attention to the basically external manifestations of Tess's and Angel's love (a natural process, despite Angel's etherealisation of Tess and Tess's turning Angel into a kind of god). Without this leisurely developed expanse, the later, starker events would be less shocking. It is only as one looks closely at the events of the Talbothays scene, and tries to place them in the novel as a whole, that one realises how few pages have been read. The substance of plot at this point in the novel may be thin, but the subtext of Tess's feelings and passages of spiritual intensity makes this a section of remarkable emotional impact.

In the first chapter of Phase the Sixth (chapter 45), the meeting with Alec makes specific the connection between the first part of Tess's life and the present: 'The break of continuity between her earlier and present existence, which she had hoped for, had not after all taken place. Bygones would never be complete bygones till she was a bygone herself' (45: 298–9). It is critical to note that this passage occurs before Alec thrusts himself back into her life. That is, had he not left the barn in which he was preaching and followed her, the same implication presumably would be present. Hardy's locating the passage before the appearance of Alec raises discrepant hypotheses: is it within Tess's consciousness that the early part of her story is made to affect the latter, finally tragic part, or is it just that this is Hardy's way of suggesting the interconnectedness of past and fate?

A traditional realistic plot would have a finely and precisely tuned concatenation of circumstances developed earlier in the story. And of course there is much of this in *Tess* as Alec and Angel and the dairymaids interact shortly before the climax. But much of this interaction is meretricious, or simply discarded by the narrator as contributing factors to the tragedy; and this obviously conscious rejection of the possibilities he had been preparing alerts the reader to Hardy's innovative — or at least doggedly independent — creation of tragic emotions.

In any event, once Alec re–enters the mix of circumstances impinging on the novel's plot, events rapidly take purposive direction. In chapter 47 Tess has struck Alec; in 48 his ready forgiveness of this blow helps prompt her impassioned letter to Angel; in 49 Angel's change of mind is chronicled and Tess is called home because her mother is near death; in chapter 50 she arrives home, she meets Alec in the Satanic scene, and her father dies (with the news of the family's being expelled); and in 51 the issue–forcing Lady–Day migration is under way.

The bodily and spiritual exhaustion induced by Tess's work on the grain thresher seems to attenuate her ability to resist Alec. Her striking him with the heavy glove and drawing blood in a manner anticipative of her next strike at him is more a sign of the desperation that precedes capitulation than it is a throw of the d'Urbervillian gauntlet, as Alec smugly recognises (' "I can make full allowance for this" . . . he said blandly' (47: 321)). The presentation here provides less an analysis of her than a portrayal of what events she takes part in, which is not only Aristotelian in principle but effectively creates a tone preceding the climactic Phase the Seventh appropriate to that Phase's presentation of Tess almost entirely from an external — Angel's — perspective.

Chapter 6

Tragedy

Although there is a tendency in twentieth–century writers, and literary critics, to approach tragedy as a high and daunting ideal, to attempt a tragedy in the nineteenth century was a frequent undertaking, and it is not surprising that, given Hardy's brooding and unflinching intellect, the genre has a powerful presence in his stories. If his success is finest and most subtle in tragedy, he had attempted and succeeded before, and his experiments continued after, *Tess of the d'Urbervilles*.

That the Victorians thought they could achieve the dignity of tragic art did not mean they devalued the genre. Far from that: they held it to be a reflector of essential qualities of their culture. Because Matthew Arnold was concerned that readers of *Empedocles on Etna* might allow the philosophy and suicide of Empedocles to affect their outlook on life, and because he felt that his age required energetic and pragmatic solutions to problems rather than meditative and self–absorbed analysis, he withdrew the poem from the second edition of his *Poems* and in the volume's famous Preface explained his motives. *Idylls of the King* is a steadily measured projection of the need in Tennyson's society for moral courage tempered by political need for action. While *The Ring and the Book* is only intermittently 'tragic', there is little question but that Browning drew upon tragic precepts in its portrayal of the Pope; Browning's knowledge of tragedy shaped several of his early dramas and poems in a more academic fashion, and the later *Balaustion's Adventure* both summarises and revises Euripides' *Alcestis*. Two of the most remarkable religious writers of the last part of the nineteenth century – John Henry Newman and Gerard Manley Hopkins – responded in diametrically opposed ways to dilemmas of choice, Newman by insisting on the inviolability of first principles, Hopkins by voicing desolate religious nega-tions; and a non-religious writer — George Eliot — incorporated within Hegelian stress and indeterminacy a demonstration of Christian tragedy in *Romola*, and translated classical precepts to a Victorian political setting in *Felix Holt*. The tragic spirit of uncompromised resoluteness in the face of basic conflict distinguishes the analytical method of Walter Pater's prose, prose which had its impact on the presentation of *Tess*.

Underlying this awareness and exploitation of the power of tragedy on the part of creative writers are layers of more-or-less academic literary thinking by journalists and by university-related dons, who in any case wrote more on Greek tragedy than on current developments. And probably influenc-ing the era's selection of tragedy as one of the dominant literary modes more than either abstract discussion or other literary works was the replacement, on several intellectual and religious levels, of pre–existing ways of thinking with 'new' ways of perceiving and judging. These latter need to be only briefly sketched for their role to be evident. (1) The decline of belief systems under the multiple impact of Higher Criticism, the re-establishment of the Catholic hierarchy (relevant only for England), and Darwinism. (2) The rise of relativism, impres-sionism, and individuality — all of which elevated the separate perception and deprecated group or conventional wisdom. Thus, conventionality as never before became a liability to 'see-ing things as they really are' and a roadblock to progress. In previous eras, convention allowed a thinker to accept unques-tioningly certain features of life and social existence, and to pro-ceed along new lines: this gives security as one moves into un-charted areas (e.g., the Industrial Revolution). In the Victorian era, the areas 'left behind' as one progresses — the beliefs and cer-tainties of society and childhood — were themselves uncertain: thus, writers are not only anxious about the future, but about the past, indeed about the conditions of one's very existence. (3) Science itself increased the sense that nothing can be known, and that nothing is stable. Pater reflects the impact of this third way of thinking perhaps more clearly than anyone else, but Pater is only expressing that which is in many people's minds.

The variety of ways tragic energies are manifested in Victorian writing suggests there was a pre-existing, receptive state of literary thinking about tragedy. Whereas in the early decades of Victoria's reign Greek *exempla* are used as models, and thus provide an aura of intellectuality and rationality, after 1860 the example of Greek tragedy became less influential (despite the growing acceptance among academic writers of Hegel's use of Greek tragedy as a focus of his analyses); and the Victorians' ideas that tragedy needed to be based on stable conditions became less sustainable. The 'decline' of Greek models as a standard occurs especially, but hardly as an isolated phenomenon, in the conservative literary and political magazine, *Blackwood's*. Tragedy became less situated in the mind, or in the rationality, and more in the emotions, that is, in the context created specifically in each work. Although reviewers' steady commentary on tragedy may be dependent upon a temporal attitude of their society, Hardy was able to exploit and undercut conventionality in *Tess*.

Traditional tragedy

Features of traditional tragedy abound in *Tess*, including the idea of universals, around which much traditional theory itself revolves. Some other features are Tess's growing in stature; the reinforcement, through mythic connections, of her extrapersonal significance; absolutism; and the (fruitful) confusion between chance and volition. But giving *Tess of the d'Urbervilles* its special aura, as opposed to generic qualities of tragedy, are Hardy's own techniques and emphases.

Despite the depth of feeling experienced by nearly everyone who reads the novel, to attempt to discuss *Tess* in relation to a conventional or traditional idea of tragedy will not do. The idea of characters' *stature* or social consequence as a determining factor in tragedy dies hard; but only part of the problem lies in Tess's humble social condition as a Durbeyfield, for, after all, she is a descendant of one of the historically powerful families in Wessex. She could be forced into a traditional definition of tragedy because of her membership in a once-proud and powerful family – but then, so could many of the other characters in the novel, and in the traditional view of tragedy the protagonist is 'special', not one of the mob. Tess falls short of nobility in another aspect of that word customarily used to define tragic elevation: a 'lack of firmness' characterises her choices and behaviour at crucial turns in her life. She falls to Alec initially with only gratitude for his buying a horse to replace Prince as an excuse; she manages to confess her past to Angel without actually getting the message to him and then marries him in spite of her knowledge that he still thinks her 'innocent'; and she returns to Alec, doubting that Angel – presumably the core of her existence – will ever come back to her.

A frequent element of tragedy, and one that is frequently explicit in definitions, is a quality of absolutism – in, for example, the protagonist's willingness, even insistence, to go to any means to achieve the end she or he is pursuing, and a refusal to compromise, to accept any variance from one's sense of self or, more broadly in tragedy, of the self's identity in the world. There may be certain conditions of this novel which one could say are 'absolute': for instance, Tess's freedom from the consequence of experience, that keeps her pure in mind and act; or her unsceptical love for Angel; or the possibility in her of a mystic consciousness that is independent of physical actuality. But for nearly all of the novel the protagonist Tess is notable not for being fixed in resolve but for an adaptability to new conditions and to fresh tests of purity.

This suggests that Tess 'begins really to exist' as a tragic character – that is, achieves the stability of a personality no longer subject to changed circumstances – only when she kills Alec. And perhaps this is true: all her previous action is a prolegomenon to this moment when she realises (albeit not consciously) that she is willing to risk all (even Angel's rejection) in order to achieve a brief period of fulfilment. Previously, of course, she had trimmed her eagerness to consummate her love in order to appease Angel (that is, to conform to society's expectations – and her own, in so far as her motives are socially determined) at their honeymoon residence, and to go uncomplainingly back to her parents when he goes to Brazil. At Sandbourne, understanding that Angel had returned, with love for her, and that unless she regains him this time she will not have another chance, she does all that is necessary to have that moment. In a real sense, she is the essence of herself − self-realisation in passion and love − from this point on.

It seems plausible also that the success of *Tess* as tragedy is dependent in part on the protagonist's being a male fantasist's dream. Not only does she accept all the pain and humiliation that Angel seems willing to dispense, but in order to achieve a brief time of reciprocated love and physical passion with Angel she sacrifices the rest of her life. If there is any justification for thinking the popularity of *Tess* is owing in good part to Tess's evident masochism (seen also in her absorbing the blame for Prince's death, quite overlooking her father's drunkenness, and allowing her mother to send her to her cousin's despite her reluctance), or at least her suffering uncomplainingly the demands made on her by those whose roles should be protective rather than exploitative (family and husband), this explanation of the novel's achievement of tragic power may also make sense.

Finally, twentieth-century perspectives upon literature and tragedy perhaps give us a quite different basis from which to respond to *Tess* than its contemporary readers had, an observation intended not to suggest the Victorians did not know how to read the literature they produced themselves, but to suggest that great literature is not produced by formula or social endorsement. It is evident that Hardy knew what he was writing in *Tess*, but that is not to say that his readers grasped it all. A striking instance of the way Hardy's vision went beyond his society's comprehension is his disavowal, in letters but also in his prefaces and occasionally in the novels themselves, of a discernible didactic purpose or consistent line of argument in his narratives. (His readers and reviewers particularly admired − and his detractors criticised − his works precisely for their forceful vision of life.)

Much tragic theory of the twentieth century rests upon the stress between opposing views. A recent student of the relationship between tragedy and the significance of life has pointed out the necessity for ambiguity and the concomitant crucial rejection of that ambiguity by the protagonist. That is, tragedy depends upon the tragic mind's not accepting ambiguity and, instead, keeping alive the demand for reason and clarity (Goldmann, 'The Tragic Vision', 295). 'The greatness of tragic man [sic] lies in the fact that he sees and recognises these opposites and inimical elements in the clear light of absolute truth, and yet never accepts that this shall be so. For if he were to accept them, he would destroy the paradox, he would give up his greatness and make do with his poverty and wretchedness' (ibid., 294). Goldmann is a Marxist critic, one of several whose studies of uncertainties and ambiguities — the contradictions between the social conditions and the characters and the social beliefs — provide an entrance into internal qualities of *Tess* (and other tragedies), which are quite distinct from a limited political programme.

Hardy's career as tragedian

From Hardy's efforts to write tragedy before he began *Tess*, it is clear — from *The Mayor of Casterbridge* as well as from *The Return of the Native* — that he had the insight and skill to install classical motifs and structures in narratives with rural and intellectually and socially simple characters; just as it is clear from *The Woodlanders* (1887) that he was able to create a tragedy of traditional patterns with other significant variations. So to think of *Tess* as a tragedy requires neither condescension nor apologetics, although it may be necessary to realise that in this novel, as in his next great story, *Jude the Obscure*, Hardy had other, and perhaps higher, aims than merely to succeed in a literary genre.

In other words, *Tess* and *Jude* are the culmination of some strains in Hardy's thinking and writing career he had felt necessary or at least wise to disguise up to that point. He had agreed to suppress his first novel, *The Poor Man and the Lady* (1868), which by all accounts and surviving evidence had been a stringent and direct attack on class prejudice and the economic squashing of aspirants of humble station. And although his political sentiments are evident in such partial areas of future novels as the contemptuous feeling by Elfride Swancourt's family for the rising architect, Stephen Smith (*A Pair of Blue Eyes*), most of the imaginative energy and narrator sympathy in his novels are directed towards meeting aesthetic aims. In *The Woodlanders* he presents social issues, with Felice Charmond and Grace Melbury both damaged (one fatally) by the disastrous aristocratic selfishness of Edred Fitzpiers; and Giles Winterborne is first humiliated and then killed by a narrow-mindedness of which he partakes as much as does his surrounding rural society, whose fate his self-slaughter in effect adumbrates.

The Mayor of Casterbridge is Hardy's most ambitious and successful effort in traditional tragedy. As Henchard declines in social position (which attracts an Oedipus-like tragic status), he rises in personal stature and in insight. He becomes more aware of others' wishes, especially Elizabeth-Jane's.

This novel, then, is both a preparation for the domestic relationship leading to tragedy in *Woodlanders*, and to the expression in *Tess* of a tragedy based on the sensitivity of the individual. In *Tess*, of course, the central character becomes conscious of her innate importance and significance, or at least the reader does, whereas in *Mayor* Henchard merely becomes conscious of humanity's claims, of *others'* reality. But the directions are similar in stressing sanctity of the individual, apart from social or class level.

A further distinction of *The Mayor of Casterbridge* among Hardy's works is its portrayal of the inherent status/stature of Henchard, reinforced by what he achieves, but essentially independent of his worldly stature; thus, even after he loses everything he retains the reader's interest. This again closely resembles Oedipus, who establishes himself in Laius' kingdom, and after the revelation exiles himself. Henchard is perhaps Hardy's only 'larger-than-life' hero (possibly excepting Eustacia, and Hardy treats her ironically).

One way of sketching the culmination of Hardy's career as a tragic novelist is that in *The Mayor of Casterbridge* he embodies traditional and nineteenth-century concepts of tragedy, and then in his later three novels branches out in technique. *The Woodlanders* offers the dignity of each individual (and there are several, each of near-equal stature and significance in the narrative), with almost offhand suggestions of Giles's traditional connections with the wood god and Melbury's social role. Thus, while tragic energy is diffused, it is also securely located not in universals but in basically unique individuals. *Tess* heightens both the role of universals and the highly specific person of Tess.

Hardy came to the writing of *Tess* with a full head of steam after deciding about six years earlier that Wessex was his subject and tragedy his genre, and in the midst of a reading and thinking programme that made him aware of latest developments in late–Victorian intellectual cogitation. By the time of *Tess* he had begun to read Schopenhauer, whom previously he had happened to echo in concept and attitude, and whose ideas he had probably become aware of through articles in quarterlies; he had become a friend of Walter Pater, whose aesthetic of evocative detail, or pointillism, is so dominant in this novel; and he had realised that the advice of Leslie Stephen and other publishers and editors of periodicals that he avoid 'offensive' topics of religion and sexuality could be more harmful than beneficial. So, while it would not be accurate to say that he wrote *Tess* with no holds barred, he did come to this novel with a more ambitious agenda and a richer reservoir of ideas and imaginative techniques than he had brought to previous novels.

Some of these ideas, which space prevents my explication dealing with, are mentalism; social and monetary exploitation of down-and-out peasantry by *nouveau riche* 'gentry'; terrorism by arrogance: intellectual adventurers without a clear sense of purpose or of social obligation (Angel); larger social/industrial/agricultural movements that proceed without concern for those persons most materially and physically and viscerally affected (threshers; swede diggers); the vacuity and haplessness of social agencies such as the Church presumably set up to help those in need, but which instead work doctrinally and careeristically; and, most complexly of all, relativism and subjectivity. An interesting speculation might be whether these concepts — in humanistic terms so admirable and desirable — might not be ultimately responsible for the suffering of such people as Tess, who are not able to incorporate such complexities into the mundaneness of their conceptions and ambitions.

The purpose of an explication of so many points would be to show how these conditions are employed to convey the kind of tragedy Hardy is working to achieve; but I think that many of these larger issues have been covered in my consideration of the underscorings and contradictions of Tess's stature, as a near-conventional portrayal of tragic potential and explicit denials that she is out of the ordinary, and more can be said about this. I would like to consider at some length how Hardy manages the intellectual and emotional establishment of Tess's stature.

Status and democracy in the novel

Hardy was not the first Victorian writer to base a tragedy on the concept of innate individual stature or upon the principles of democracy. It is a necessity of mimetic fiction to employ greater specificity in establishing the identity of a character on a page, in order to overcome the absence of the concrete presence of an actor on a stage. This necessity plays against another aspect of the very nature of writing, which makes every character representative, or the bearer of a value system or a 'meaning'. Prior to Hardy, the English novelist who melds these two aspects of fiction to produce tragedy most successfully is George Eliot, whose Maggie Tulliver is more individualised and more free from intellectualised connections with her society than Tess. But while *The Mill on the Floss* is a wonderful evocation of the pain of achieving a self-identity in a society founded on roles, Eliot is less successful with the novel's structure, with a climax that rejects the entire drift of the narrative's logic. Maggie's progress towards identity is cut short by the flood — as if neither she nor her creator were able to conceive an existence that either expressed love or declared love was unattainable.

What Hardy does is to shape the reader's knowledge of the personality of the tragic sufferer throughout the novel, concerned not to establish consistency or a character 'line', not even concerned to make her an independent or forceful character as one might expect in a tragedy, but to create a full portrait of her possibilities of experience. This portrait is shaped by a context suggestive of universals as well as specific and transitory features of Tess herself. To describe Hardy's achievement thus does not, of course, convince: only through a reading of the novel can the effect of Hardy's interweaving of event, character, and narrator analysis be felt. And 'feeling' is his secret of creating tragedy in *Tess of the d'Urbervilles*. But my aim here is to provide some guidance, mostly through selecting and discussing relevant passages.

The foundation for Hardy's idea of tragedy of the individual pervades the novel. One strong aspect of this is the discovery of the essential uniqueness of each 'Hodge' in the rural environs. Perhaps the clearest generalised presentation of the individual is in Pascal's statement quoted by Hardy, a translation of which is: 'The sharper one's mind, the more one notices how many original men there are; the common run of people do not notice differences between men.' And, at the end of the paragraph containing Pascal's epigraph, the partial quotation from *Macbeth* emphasises the point: 'men every one of whom walked in his own individual way the road to dusty death' (18: 123). Obviously, the point is that tragedy is universal, open to the willingness and capacity to perceive the common lot.

The concomitant emphasis is upon Tess's special quality through intermittent reminders, such as Tess as 'visionary essence of woman' (20: 134). Earlier she had been the 'standard woman' (14: 96). In both of these there is the blending of Tess as one against whom others are measured, and of Tess as the average. In chapter 20, presumably Angel's generalising tendency affects his perception; none the less, Tess is being presented as combining tragic extremism of individuality and of general significance. In herself she is Dionysian and Apollonian.

As 'a visionary essence of woman – a whole sex condensed into one typical form', Tess is intended to suggest the tragic extremism of individuality. But Hardy is clearly determined not to permit Tess to transcend for long the actuality which causes her to suffer. Shortly after Angel sees her as the 'visionary essence of woman' – with what degree of authorial compliance we are left to surmise – the narrator notes that in brighter light of day she becomes 'simply feminine', changing from 'a divinity who could confer bliss to . . . a being who craved it' (20: 135).

It is clear that Hardy strongly emphasises the democracy of tragedy: there can be no mistake about this being his intention. This novel's credo of the worth of the individual differs from that which shapes *The Mayor of Casterbridge*, for instance, although there, too, conventional stature is displaced onto an almost accidental mayor of a provincial county town.

It is the situation at Talbothays that allows Hardy to develop his concept of specialness amidst ordinariness the most fully. Tess is initially indistinguishable to Angel from the other dairymaids, and the milkmaids' love for Angel is described in terms that could have been applied to Tess's relationship with Alec, as opposing social, but not natural law (23: 149); their love is a contrast between civilisation (it is unjustified) and Nature (perfectly plausible). Whatever judgement we may be inclined to make about Tess's falling to Alec, the other milkmaids would be less likely to resist Angel had he been of Alec's inclinations. Their desire of him is stronger than 'practicalities' (24: 154). Their deportment – knowing they cannot win him, in the face of their 'killing joy' – gives them a 'resignation, a dignity', which in Hardy no less than in Eliot is a tragic concept, permitting the dairymaids to partake of a significant thematic tension. The novel's bias demands there be no special valorisation of Tess, but at the same time Tess steadily is made to rise out of the background. At one point, for example, Hardy suggests that Tess's more 'impassioned' nature marks her as superior to the other dairymaids, though 'in the eyes of propriety' she is less worthy of him than they (23: 149–50).

The achievement of tragedy through structure

So far, so good, in that Hardy intellectualises to a striking degree the groundwork for the kind of tragedy that is being developed. Once this groundwork is established — once the reader has been inundated with information and views that stress Tess's mundaneness and yet her extraordinariness merely in being human — he relies on structure for the emotional impact. It is crucial, for example, that the section on Talbothays is as extended as it is, as I have argued in chapter 5. Without this leisurely developed expanse, the later, starker events in Phases the Fifth and Sixth would be less shocking, less disturbing in their implications of the limited possibilities of existence, and the horror of Phase the Seventh would be on the level of melodrama. For clearly, there is a society which can accommodate Tess's past. Perhaps more to the point, the long interval at Talbothays suggests in brilliant imagery and scenes that Tess is so close to happiness — if only Angel had been 'more a man, less a spirit'. That is the pain and anguish of her story. Tess merely does what a human does — she works, finds a person to love, and is ready to move on to the other mundane activities of life. And she is suddenly, starkly derailed, by a surging reminder of the arbitrariness of the options of behaviour allowable in the larger society within which most persons' happiness is to be found; and the derailment is highlighted by Angel's being guilty of precisely the same 'sin' as Tess — which emphasises how narrowly Tess had missed her chance.

At the end of the section at Talbothays, characterisations have been established, the 'society' which has judged Tess and which presumably will be judging her in the future portions has been seen both to have general, if temporal, standards and individualised voices. Phase the Fourth completes the initiatory part of the novel. A little more than half the novel has been presented, and from this point the tone shifts substantially. The first part of the novel illustrates a variety of ways society accommodates sexual instinct. In terms of class distinctions, no one expects Alec to marry Tess, no one would be surprised if Angel acted toward Tess as Alec has done. Alec's drive for physical sexuality is not markedly different from Tess's: although she feels Angel's moral, intellectual, and social superiority, and although she idolises him, she also is interested in physical possession. Angel may be more light than fire, but he also can show strong physical emotion, as is shown when he comes across the space in the field and impulsively embraces Tess.

Thus, the first half of the novel portrays the conflict between society and nature on a fairly straightforward level. What the second half does is to fulfil the direst possibilities of the first half, in a way that emphasises the artificiality of society. In other words, Angel's hypocrisy and his acceptance of the double standard impel the events of the second half.

The forms of society are so well accepted that Tess herself scarcely seriously attacks his hypocrisy. The first part of the novel shows how thoroughly these forms are embodied in day-to-day life, and implies that they are pliable, open to humane modification. These points are suggested both in Joan's attitude (a lot of people do it, and husbands learn to live with it) and in the attitude of the field folk (she was more sinned against than sinning). It is the second half which portrays these forms in their virulence, present in Angel in a perverse, blind fashion, harmful to him; coloured by the shading imagery of Flintcomb-Ash and Stonehenge; projected in the wanderings of Tess. Contrary to her essential voluntary changes of location in the first half of the novel, in the second half she is driven from point to point, pursued by the 'scandal' of being separated from her husband, by her own need for punishment, by a combination of grief and loyalty directed at Angel, and finally by her family.

A further reflection upon the parts of the novel as tragedy might be that in the first half of the novel Tess is trying in effect to 're-establish' her virginity even though she has no conscious intention of finding another mate; that is, she accommodates herself in the world. In the second half, her own feelings and beliefs combine with those of her society to give her few options of self-realisation until, finally, in bitter desperation, she insists upon self-realisation above all other possibilities.

A point important to recognise about the tragic impact of *Tess* is that although tragedy culminates in Phase the Seventh, the novel does not demonstrate steady linear development of her character, nor does its protagonist steadily stand up to the forces that work against her. For eight months after Angel departs for Brazil, Tess maintains her Talbothays consciousness, 'in utter stagnation'. That is, she does not become more reflective, analytical, or critical of the way things are. This passivity underscores the kind of tragic figure Tess is: the impact she makes is controlled more by situation than by her comprehension. In a certain way this may be Aristotelian (however astounded Aristotle might be to find his views on plot applied to a novel rather than to a play), but more significantly it means that her main claim to tragic stature lies in her ability to accept what happens to her without resistance, and this is not customarily judged to be a tragic quality. Her resistance is intermittent, occasional, and situation-specific, suggesting again that Tess is not a characteristic tragic figure.

This point is emphasised frequently by reminders of the schism between Tess's 'understanding' of an issue and the way in which that understanding affects — or more frequently does not affect — her conduct. The narrator makes it clear that Tess understands the relativity of social and natural law, but also indicates that she cannot 'rise high enough to despise opinion . . . so long as [that opinion] was held by Clare' (42: 272). Tess thus does 'know' true values, but is too weak and human to live by that knowledge. The need to redefine tragedy as it works in *Tess* is that Tess by now 'knows' tragically — that is, the dislocation of human life in the natural and social universe, and the contradictions created by the survival of aspects of nature in acculturated humanity; and a traditional tragic character would, like Henchard in *Mayor*, decline to struggle further and perhaps even take steps to move out of life. But Tess, quite unheroically and individually, as opposed to microcosmically, remains subject to the whims of a very fallible single human being. One cannot conceive of Antigone submitting her views of what is eternally required by divine law to the judgement of Creon, her fiancé, or either of her brothers. *Tess* may embody a conflict of principles, true enough, but one of those principles is open only to individual evaluation – i.e., to romantic love.

It is, thus, the very ordinariness of Tess which finally constitutes her stature. She has already pleaded with Angel not to make her suffer a punishment greater than she can bear – which instantly separates her from such as Henchard, Hardy's comparably dominating male character. Her references in her letter to Angel to 'temptation', and her acknowledgement that the punishment he has 'measured out' is 'deserved', clearly correlate with the idea of moral and tragic balance, but Tess asks not for justice but for kindness. She refers to herself as 'poor me' (48: 325). It is clear that Tess is not positing herself as a tragic figure; rather, she deliberately rejects that sort of austerity in favour of personal fulfilment. Her mundane human interest in happiness, which has survived essentially unmodified ever since the wedding night until this point, is what gives much poignance to the novel's final events. That is, circumstances conspire so that it is only with murder, only by taking irretrievable steps, that she is able to gain the position or status through which she can achieve what she perceives, without articulating it in this manner, to be self-fulfilment and self-identity – i.e., what she has wanted all along, simple emotional and physical congress with Angel.

The point that is developed in the description of Tess's reaction to Angel, who has suddenly re-appeared in the Sandbourne lodging-house, is not that Tess at this crisis in her life is behaving or is going to behave 'nobly' or heroically. It is not on this level of 'tragedy' that the novel has its force. The point is that Tess is behaving in the only way she is able, because, with her defences against sexual 'impurity' reduced and with her sense of family responsibility finally become oppressive, she can only behave in the way that she 'is', and that is beyond right and wrong, or justice or revenge. By the circumstances of physical life that includes male pursuit of the female, by the limitations of her personal situation that includes a set of ne'er-do-well parents and a society that places a 'use value' on her, as well as by the mysterious intractable connection that spans time and invokes moral as much as biological entities, and that curses her through her d'Urberville ancestors' behaviour — by all these she has been prevented from achieving the most elemental kind of happiness, the kind that comes through physical intimacy based on affection. It is this that she must have for her identity; it is this that, both in leaving Trantridge and in the murder at the Sandbourne lodging-house, is the effective cause of her casting aside her self-devaluation that made her Alec's thing; it is this, finally, on which rests Tess's tragic status. This emphasis on Tess's natural sexuality suggests the relevance of Peter Brooks's linking of plot with 'desire' and the search for identity.

Described in this manner, *Tess* seems perhaps extraordinarily romantic, sentimental, and bathetic — not to mention sexist, in the clear implication that by herself, prevented from this sort of union with a man, Tess feels herself incomplete — lacking an identity, and ceasing to think of her own body as hers — and indeed unworthy. It is not at all clear that Hardy realises that his views about an emotion-founded sexual union might be skewed in the direction of suggesting that the male is more crucial to the woman's sense of self than vice versa. But in any event, in his next novel, *Jude*, he compensates for any imbalance of this sort by simply inverting the situation. I do not deny that *Tess* may be sexist in this manner, however firm and devastating may be Hardy's unpacking and dismantling of the Victorian double-standard in the confession scene on their wedding night through its grotesque satire of Angel's miming his society's insistence upon feminine purity whatever may be the history of his own morality. But my intention is neither to endorse nor to excuse the novel's hidden sexual politics. Many current feminists' ambivalent admiration for the novel is distinguished by objection to its complacent and condescending descriptions of the gender-based culture/nature dichotomy and by acknowledgement of the stark clarity of culture's twin cruelties towards women in Angel and Alec; it seems to me

that this ambivalence is evidence also of Hardy's refusal to portray gender behaviour from a single perspective.

What Hardy accomplishes, then, is a kind of Grecian austerity, but in terms of a domestic and personal situation, not
founded on a universal principle. This domestic and limited
perspective is reinforced when, in response to wondering how
she might make herself more acceptable to Angel should he
return, Tess tries to learn some of Angel's favourite songs, as
far as anyone can remember what they were (49: 331). Here,
as frequently, Tess shows herself to be practical, non-reflective,
and somewhat limited in her ability to make an imaginative
leap into Angel's more abstract concerns. This, of course,
emphasises that Tess's tragedy involves a specific case, not
merely a generalisable situation.

The 'success' of Tess's character depends upon its having
no point of rest or stability, of finality. She is in a novel in
which the various levels of language and the use of symbols,
actions, and reflection evade circumscribed definition.
Arguably, she comes close to the traditional posture of tragic
rebellion at the point when she writes her bitter note to Angel,
which is prefatory (although not intentionally so on Tess's part)
to her rejoining Alec. Tess's saying she does not deserve her
punishment is her rebellion against injustice. But the manner
of the letter is inherently contradictory, and within context it
is incoherent, expressing Tess's lack of self-knowledge — she
'passionately' scribbles the condemnatory letter to Angel,
although in that letter she says she has 'thought it all over
carefully' (51: 343). The note is her chance to verbalise her self,
and in one sense it does, conveying a self that reacts vehemently
to the moment rather than to timeless ideals. That this com-
plaint against Angel's conduct occurs at the moment of her
greatest leaning to Alec adds an ironic aspect to her situation.
These contradictions undercut Tess as a traditional tragic hero;
but, of course, they substantiate a claim that she is a development or an experiment in tragedy.

Phase the Seventh: fulfilment

Phase the Seventh is an immensely rich and complex culmination of the novel's various and sometimes conflicting concerns:
the cohesion of Tess's murder of Alec and her own death with
Hardy's structuring the book on social themes and morality,
on aesthetic subtleties and strong directness, creates an impact
rare in fiction. There are different concepts of the most effective form of tragedy. Critics of Shakespeare suggest that he
placed his climax in the centre of the play, with the final two
acts (as the plays are divided by editors) portraying the consequence of the actions taken in the third act. In many Greek
tragedies the tragic act has occurred before the presentation
begins, at Aulis, at the crossroads where Oedipus kills Laius,
or at the point where he marries the widowed queen. With
modern narratives the tragedy tends to occur late in the
action, so that action-consequence-revelation can occur almost
simultaneously. Such is the case with *Tess*, with emphases upon
aspects of the situation that further suggest the modernity of
Hardy's conception. While Phase the Seventh could not have
its power without Hardy's careful preparation, one can also
examine this Phase as the epitome of Hardy's concept. In much
the way that adumbration operates from the first scene in the
plot to carry the reader forward, so in a significant sense Phase
the Seventh rehearses all of the preceding novel's preparation
for it.

That concept involves the deliberate elision of traditional
methods and implications. The tragedy Hardy aims to achieve
is a tragedy of ordinary persons with ordinary hopes, whose
grandeur is located in the insistence of fulfilment, whatever
the cost.

Most noticeable in establishing this sort of tragedy are
developments in Hardy's treatment of elevation. Although the
characters are fairly clearly seen as combatting powerful forces,
they remain solidly mundane. For most of this Phase Hardy
simply discards the idea of Tess's specialness he had
been working on, however ambivalently. When Mrs Clare —
with seemingly uncharacteristic arrogance — says about her

daughter-in-law that Angel should not 'be so anxious about a mere child of the soil!' (53: 356), Hardy may be suggesting how class affects the British sense of humanity. Angel reveals that Tess is of an old Norman family. This is supposed to be his trump card in reconciling his family to his marriage, but he throws it away here; and in fact nothing is made of it either by him or his parents, except that he notes that many agricultural families in 'our villages' have similar backgrounds. Clearly, whatever had led Hardy in the course of revising the first version of his story to emphasise Tess's being a descendant of the d'Urbervilles (see Grindle and Gatrell's 'Introduction' to their edition of *Tess 25–9*; and see Laird *The Shaping of 'Tess of the d'Urbervilles'* 109–17) he did not think it critical enough to make her residual social status a major element in the plot at the narrative's approaching climax and denouement. The deletion of this novel-long motif is one element which directs the attentive reader towards a more non-mythic, a more visceral and immediate energy at the core of Tess's tragedy than the classical resonances of family and social consequence.

Similarly, there is a sudden slowing and even denial of the tragic aggrandisement of the force of events. Angel's cautious behaviour when he first arrives home from Brazil is deflating. The first description of Angel's mood upon arriving at home shows his fear that Tess may speak impolitely to him in front of her parents, and so he dawdles a day or two before rereading her letter, and the paragraph repeated in the novel's text is the one in which she begs him to be 'a little kind' and to 'Come to me, come to me, and save me from what threatens me!' (53: 358).

Most remarkable of all, in terms of the accretion of tragic power, just preceding his departure, and coming at the final point in the chapter, is the reference to the letter from Marian and Izz: it is presented offhandedly as 'also lately come to hand', but obviously the letter had not hurried Angel. This confluence of information, as well as the month it had taken Marian and Izz to write their note in the first place, creates uncertainty as to exactly when Tess agreed to become

Alec's mistress, and thus whether, had either the women or Angel acted more promptly, Tess might have had a different fate.

A further deflation of traditional tragic connotation is the manner in which the new residents of the Durbeyfields's cottage have no interest in their predecessors (54: 359), suggesting the lack of societal significance in Tess's existence or background. The description of them underscores Hardy's pragmatic 'theory' of tragedy in this novel, stressing relativity in terms close to those about Sorrow, the bearing relativity has on passages describing tragedy made explicit: 'talking as though the time when Tess lived there were not one whit intenser in story than now'. In short, this description defines a good part of the way the novel establishes its context of tragedy.

This aspect of the novel makes *Tess of the d'Urbervilles* a different sort of tragedy from such works as *Oedipus Rex, Hamlet, King Lear*, and *Anna Karenina*. These works' impact does not depend upon cross-purposes in the sense of coincidences: their results are inevitable, given the works' premises. In *Tess*, on the other hand, it is manifestly evident that, although Tess conceives herself and other occupants of the world to be better off dead than alive, the specific disasters that befall her are all linked to temporality − either the temporality of the morality that condemns Tess or the temporal interrelationships of connected events. Thus Hardy creates irony on a smaller scale than does Sophocles; and the effect if less grandiose and dignified is more painful: if only human beings could respond more quickly to educative moments in their lives and could apply their fresh insights more immediately to their own and others' lives, suffering could be averted.

To Hardy tragedy is immediate, contiguous, and specific, and its remedies are pragmatic, and come within the scope of normal decent human effort. The most profound consequences and human emotions are open to the experience of the humblest citizen. If indeed *Tess* is one of the greatest fifty books of the last century − as periodical writers used to claim − one of the bases of this placement is in its disintegration of the idea of the elite.

Phase the Seventh is the point of highest achievement in tragedy in *Tess*, and it is worth pointing out that its tone is in keeping with the previous phases of the novel. Hardy has prepared things well enough, so that he does not here have to strain to reach tragedy. As with the rape/seduction scene, Hardy does not grant direct access to the critical tragic act in this part of the novel, the moment of Tess's return to Alec. The tone of several passages suggests that Tess may have given herself to Alec out of gratitude, not out of forced *quid pro quo*. When Angel finds her in Sandbourne, she tells Angel she hates Alec *now*, because he had lied in saying that Angel would not return (55: 366), a statement which suggests that her initial feelings upon returning to Alec had not been all negative, and in turn that his enticements had not been entirely coercive. Tess's response to her family's dilemma does not seem to present a traditional tragic situation. But it repeats the novel's oscillatory movements.

The interplay between ordinariness and grandeur continues to define the tragic element in the novel. The level of the characters' consciousness is more that of immediacy and particularity than of grandeur; but grandeur is not lost sight of. Hardy may be denying the concept of an elite, but he still employs traditional details and features of tragedy in Phase the Seventh. There are many of these — sharpening the impact of *peripeteia* or discovery by presenting Angel's preparedness to see Tess in a milkmaid's or servant's role, rather than as someone's mistress (55: 363); Tess's acceptance of eventual capture in the traditionally tragic formulation 'What must come will come' (58: 376); upon awakening at Stonehenge to find the police there, she echoes Aeschylus in saying, 'It is as it should be!' (59: 381); and Tess's last words in the novel, 'I am ready' (59: 382). Only a few passages suggest a significance beyond the individual, as with the eavesdropping landlady hearing from the drawing-room of Tess's and Alec's apartment a sound of 'one syllable,' in a 'low note of moaning, as if it came from a soul bound to some Ixionian wheel' – a 'murmur of unspeakable despair' (56: 367, 368). In the generally naturalistic scene of Phase the Seventh, this particular classical allusion has a powerful effect. In this scene of strong and most direct emotion Hardy by means of the allusion diverts the reader away from direct empathy. To put it differently, he provides a context for Tess's climactic suffering, directly associating his rural, quotidian sufferer with the mythological Ixion being punished in 'hell' by being tied to a revolving wheel. (It is interesting that the Ixionian wheel is one of Schopenhauer's favourite classical images.) If previously the narrator has occasionally evoked ideas of tragedy and suggested Tess as a tragic sufferer, here the narrator makes the connection explicit precisely in the scene where she commits the 'tragic' (because irreversible and irrevocable) act, an act which is a strong move to resolve her dilemma (which in itself is also irresolvable and irrevocable). None the less, such an association of Wessex character with expansive grandeur is restricted. An appropriate naturalisation is performed upon such an allusion by Tess herself. She associates herself with Stonehenge, through her mother, a shepherd, and through Angel's once saying she was a 'heathen': 'So now I am at home' (58: 379). Far from emphasising a revenge image, her priestess status in a prehistoric religion, or an extensive mythological resonance, Tess's manner of associating herself with a place is pragmatic, even wry, and thereby, of course, much more effective and distancing than had Hardy employed a narratorial perspective here. He is able thereby to create tragic resonance without losing the sense of his protagonist as an ordinary woman.

What develops in the course of this Phase is crucial to the success of Tess as a tragic protagonist, and to *Tess of the d'Urbervilles* as a tragic novel. Several patterns developed over the length of the novel are drawn upon again. For example, Tess responds to Angel's presence at Sandbourne and his queries with 'It is too late!'; 'Too late, too late!'; 'But I say, I say, it is too late' (58: 365). This iteration helps make

Hardy's point that the novel is structured on time − on past and present, on rural vs modern urban; on timeless behaviour vs temporal morality; on Tess as rural woman and modern. Also the novel's mentalist quality is suggested in 'Speech was as *in*expressive as silence' (55: 366; emphasis added), the negative quality of any explicit means of communication. This is a sort of non-mysticism in a context that can only exist on a mystical level; and what it points to in tragedy is much the same as the garden scene pointed to in human consciousness: that which is beyond communication; that is, its presence is determinable by its impact, but to attempt to define it is to destroy it (cf. Cave, *Recognition*). Here, it is the negativity of communication that is stressed. What is being communicated is impossibility − that is, the frustration and disappointment of both Tess and Angel.

As it had so often before, Tess's dreamlike condition occurs again in the last phase of the novel, with particularly dire results. When Angel first sees Tess in Sandbourne, she feels 'like a fugitive in a dream' (55: 365). Angel perceives that 'his original Tess had spiritually ceased to recognize' that her body is 'hers − allowing it to drift, like a corpse upon the current, in a direction dissociated from its living will', and she says that she did not care what Alec did with her (55: 366).

Her condition at this stage of her crisis-filled life is nearly a direct reminder of the rape/seduction dilemma. It also plays a variation on the motif as to Tess's having two selves − one that is 'real' and one that is Angel's conception or idealisation of her − in a peculiarly enriching manner: the 'living will' is clearly that of the emotionally vital and pure Tess, while the 'corpse' is, precisely, that of the body only, which in this con-figuration is the insignificant part of 'Tess'. Things that hap-pen to the body or corpse do not affect that part of Tess which is truly living − neither Alec's sexual violations nor the physical agony of farm work.

What this suggests, of course, is a Manichean division bet-ween good and evil, in which the spiritual or spirit is 'good' and the physical is evil − an odd connotation in this novel, which presents so much physical activity, details of farm work and rural procedures, and natural details. And of course this is an oversimplified dichotomy, nor is it entirely a correct one: for instance, Angel's spiritual adherences and his father's and brothers' lives of the mind/spirit clearly are not seen as good. In order that what is spiritualised is seen to be good it seems to need an inherent relation with the physical, as Tess has throughout, in a way best seen in the mystical garden scene, although the relation is similar in the last Phase's 'honeymoon' section, where physical union takes place within the spiritual conjunction of Tess and Angel.

Their meeting at Sandbourne is the emotional highpoint, and perhaps the 'tragic' culmination, of the narrative. It presents a dilemma from which they cannot escape in terms of their personal selves and surrounding circumstances. They seem to recognise this: 'They stood, fixed, their baffled hearts looking out of their eyes with a joylessness pitiful to see. Both seemed to implore something to shelter them from reality' (55: 366).

Hardy's presentation here suggests again the mystical motif; but more to the point is that this moment is a retreat from the concept that tragedy involves large issues, comprehended and duly put in a proper perspective, unless the point which is being 'comprehended' is that life is too complex and dreadful to be comprehended and accepted. Of particular note is that both wish to evade reality. What Tess's and Angel's tragedy initially celebrates, then, is not comprehension and acceptance but a refusal to comprehend. But, although Angel remains essentially blank, it would appear that, upstairs in Alec's and her living quarters, Tess may have 'comprehended' the necessity of murder if she is to achieve the needs of her life.

Her awareness remains almost constantly mundane, not exalted. Preceding her murder of Alec, she declares to him that she has lost Angel forever ('he will not love me the littlest bit ever any more'); that Angel will die from her sin, and that Alec had made her what she had prayed in pity not to be made again. She attacks him after 'more and sharper words' from him (56: 368). After the murder, Tess tells Angel she killed Alec because 'I owed it to you, and to myself, Angel . . . for the trap he set for me in my simple youth, and his wrong to you through me.' This way of putting it underscores the specificness of the motivation for the murder: not grandiose motivation, but pragmatic, individual. 'He has come between us and ruined us, and now he can never do it any more.' She thinks that Angel could forgive her now that she has killed Alec (57: 372) — which is, of course, a simple-minded reminder of Angel's lament, when he had first heard of Tess's past, 'If he were dead it might be different' (36: 239) — a lament whose ironic fulfilment is but one of the many ways in which Hardy simultaneously mocks and honours Tess's comprehension of values.

Another way in which Tess's tragedy is individualised is the conclusion to her blaming Alec: 'O God — I can't bear this! — I cannot!' (56: 368). This allusion to tragedy testing an individual's final resources is more indirect than the allusion to Ixion's wheel, but the educated reader — to whom Hardy obviously is appealing via his literary and artistic allusions — would respond to this, however subconsciously. Of course, in saying she cannot bear what is happening, Tess is demonstrating a non-traditional tragic posture. The classical tragic hero takes a tragic choice precisely because she or he can 'bear' it, in the sense of fully comprehending and accepting the conditions of life. With Tess, on the contrary, the criterion once again seems to be one of specific and identifiable limitations. Quite possibly, what Hardy is doing here is underscoring Tess's allegiance to her social class. That is, if Hardy grants the position that tragic suffering presupposes a certain social status — which seems to be the case in *The Return of the Native* and *The Mayor of Casterbridge*, allowing that the social elevation is in terms of local standing — with the character of Tess he deliberately refuses to have her behave in the psychologically profound manner of an Oedipus, who chooses the symbolically superb method of self-punishment of self-blinding and self-exile, or in the magnificently self-detached and committed manner of an Antigone. Instead, she remains specifically the individual Tess, representative of nothing but the will to happiness, a happiness she defines in her own terms, of having Angel.

However, I need to acknowledge that even Hardy, with this view of the crucial importance of the speckled individual, has made Tess more than a purely and limitedly naturalistic 'tragic' heroine. By providing her with an uncontrollable mystic potential, he associates Tess with considerations larger than herself – if not with objectivity, with a conception of existence that gives high place precisely to the unique spirit of the individual, an individuality which, although it can be elevated to the unity of mysticism, remains deeply bound with the sensuous perceptiveness and responsiveness of the person experiencing the feeling. Again, Tess in the garden scene had conveyed these dual and contradictory attributes.

This sort of tragic character can legitimately be shot through with limitations, for ordinary humanity with its acculturations is not made inadequate by a higher vision. Thus, when Tess lachrymosely refers to Angel as 'My own true husband' (56: 368), the reader may be perceiving Tess accurately in her self-deception, but this does not diminish the impact of her lament. Indeed, if I am correct in thinking that Tess's appeal is precisely in her long suffering and devotion to Angel in spite of his own shortcomings, this reference to him as a 'true husband', when the novel has demonstrated he has scarcely begun to learn the meaning of the word 'husband', only enhances her image in the reader's mind and emotions.

A consideration concerning the effect or impact of tragedy is that after Tess and Angel meet, with the culmination in the discovery of the dead Alec, several pages are given to their reunion, flight, sexual consummation, and apprehension. Thus *Tess* has a somewhat more diffuse impact than many tragedies (e.g., *Hamlet*) where the denouement follows nearly immediately upon the climax or tragic event. Countering this aspect of diffusion is the accumulating tension brought about by their flight and their ensconcement in the mansion, as the reader along with Tess awaits the inevitable.

Both the mundaneness of the focus of tragic energy, and Tess's self-identity being wrapped up in Angel, are repeated in Tess's willingness to be captured and executed. Tess says, 'I fear that what you think of me now may not last – I do not wish to outlive your present feeling for me . . . so that it

may never be known to me that you despised me.' Tess is
not interested in matters of principle or long-term consequence,
but solely in matters affecting her own period of consciousness.
In this she reflects modernity. Likewise, she does not employ
a timeless standard to defend her actions. She says that 'considering what my life has been I cannot see why any man
should, sooner or later, be able to help despising me' (58:
376–7). In other words, Tess still accepts the temporal social
code, although she no longer lets it control her actions: this
is in fact a strong measure of her tragic stature, in that she
rejects that which she 'accepts' as necessity.

Tess's asking Angel whether he thinks they shall meet again
after death is in keeping with her obsession with him: 'I wanted
so to see you again – so much, so much! What – not even
you and I Angel, who love each other so well?' (58: 380). One
might object to this appeal to a religious concept as Hardy's
'milking' an emotional moment, but I see it as underscoring
the personal aspect of Tess's tragedy: that is, she is raising the
claim of personal intensity. An accusation of sentimentality
misinterprets Hardy's intention. One of the novel's perpetual
contradictions is that although the impact of the narrative is
based precisely on Tess's highly individualistic quality of life
and on her individualistic claim to the total importance of her
existence, the practical effectiveness of this sort of claim is
checked by the power of opposing forces. There is a measure
of authority that does not acquiesce to the insistence made in
such a variety of ways in the novel that individualism is
supreme; neither nature's nor society's laws operate in consideration of the special, irresistible needs of identity and
fulfilment that define an individual. Thus, in providing a
dimension of self-refutation of the source of his novel's power,
Hardy is also amplifying its resonance. Tess's suffering is at
once highly personal and irrefutably universal.

' "Justice" was done, and the President of the Immortals (in
Aeschylean phrase) had ended his sport with Tess. And the
d'Urberville knights and dames slept on in their tombs unknowing' (59: 384). This famous statement, added in revision,

provides a sweep to the novel's denouement, a judgement of aesthetic dimension to the novel as a whole, and underscores the centrality to the novel of the ancient d'Urbervilles. As does Angel, Hardy has a serious use for the ancient family – a reminder both of time and of cyclic occurrence – but also of the irrelevance of the d'Urbervilles in the modern world. Their 'unknowing' underscores the contradictoriness of the novel's motifs: we pay them close heed, and at the end they are dismissed, both by Aeschylus and by time/history. The end of the novel, then, underscores the 'correctness' of Tess's 'philosophy' or drive to self-identity, for self-realisation, especially centred as it is for Tess in sexuality, is all the permanence and value to human existence there is.

The novel's concluding image, of Angel and Lizu-Lu joining hands and going 'as soon as they had strength' (59: 384), is one of attenuation after Tess's energy and courage and ability to endure. It is a rate of existence at a lower level that the novel prognosticates after Tess. And of course this is all right, since tragedy posits something unusual in the tragic actor(s), so when they are removed what is left is a reduction. Society does not move in the direction of improvement or increased strength, but of finality. Surviving characters continue to exist, but their existences do not elevate.

Chapter 7

The influence of *Tess*

Tess was published at the beginning of the last decade of the nineteenth century. It was a time of considerable intellectual and social ferment, when literary forms were being experimented with. Social conventions were being stretched by some, vigorously defended by others. It is not surprising that *Tess* was controversial, although novelists like Grant Allen portrayed sexual freedom more radically than Hardy. Many reviewers recognised the novel as Hardy's 'greatest' (William Watson, in the *Academy*) and his 'most powerful' (R. H. Hutton, in the *Spectator*), praising the force of Hardy's characterisations and Tess's dilemma, and believing the difference between this and his earlier stories its 'profound moral earnestness' (Clementina Black, in the *Illustrated London News*). Most of these also saw in the novel imperfections and qualities which would bring upon its author's head recriminations and blame. Other reviewers inclined more directly towards blame, expressing irritation, outrage, and disgust. Andrew Lang objected to the bitterness in the novel's concluding slur on the wicked and malignant 'President of the Immortals' − partly because it is insincere if Hardy does not believe in such a being; Lang also found the language used in relation to the rural classes inappropriately classical and learned. (It is Lang to whom Hardy refers ironically in the Preface to the 'Fifth Edition' as a reviewer 'who turned Christian for half–an–hour the better to express his grief that a disrespectful phrase about the Immortals should have been used' (5).) One anonymous review which angered Hardy was contemptuous of the idea of calling Tess 'pure' when she went 'back at the first opportunity to her seducer, a coarse sensual brute for whom she had never professed to feel anything but dislike and contempt', and declared that 'Mr. Hardy has told an extremely disagreeable story in an extremely disagreeable manner', parading 'Tess's sensual qualifications for the part of heroine'. Later years revealed this reviewer to be Mowbray Morris, the editor of *Macmillan's Magazine*, who had refused the chance to publish the novel because he felt the reader was kept in a lubricious state of mind in anticipation of the seduction.

Contemporary reviewers saw in *Tess* an attack upon contemporary mores; and their judgements of the novel fairly directly reflected their degree of tolerance and openmindedness. D. F. Hannigan argued that 'There is no coarseness in it, no nastiness of detail, and yet nothing essential is avoided'; he linked its author with Balzac, Nathaniel Hawthorne, and George Eliot, and claimed *Tess* is 'more deep and poignant than anything that either Zola or Guy de Maupassant has written'. Margaret Oliphant praised it for its wonderful evocation of rural life – its 'living, breathing scene,' its 'good brown soil and substantial flesh and blood, the cows, and the mangel-wurzel, and the hard labour of the fields', and admired Tess as 'a country girl of an extraordinary elevated and noble kind'; she criticises the novel not for its portrayal of sexuality but for implausibilities. She did not believe that a 'pure-minded and spotless' girl 'brought up in the extraordinary freedom and free-speaking of rural life' would have risked the ruin of her reputation by riding away with Alec merely to escape the teasing of the other servants, or that she would have either gone back to Alec at the end or killed him. (The poetic qualities of *Tess* may have blunted her and others' responses. Hardy's next novel left few opportunities to see potential beauties in harsh lives, and the outcry was much more fierce than with *Tess*. Mrs Oliphant placed the author of *Jude* with Grant Allen and several unnamed contemporary novelists as members of 'The Anti-Marriage League', bitterly accusing Hardy of coarse indecency in portraying the relations of Jude and Arabella, and of a desire to have physical relations replace love as the foundation of society's basic institution, marriage.)

Among Hardy's peers there were both admiration and disdain for *Tess*. George Moore thought the novel excessively

fanciful and unrealistic and poetic. His characteristic response
was to rewrite the novel, in the way that it should have been
done. He called the result *Esther Waters*. Esther is seduced by
a fellow servant, and is discharged when her pregnancy is
noticed. She struggles to support herself and her son. She surrenders the opportunity to marry a forgiving, religious man
in order to live with and eventually marry the boy's father, to
whom she is still attracted. She nurses her husband through
his final illness, and finally becomes the companion to her first
employer, now a widow and impoverished, and is consoled by
the love of her son, who has become a soldier. Moore's style
in this novel is direct and realistic — none of the characters
has much imagination or intensity — a corrective to what he
considered the excessive romanticism of Hardy's style. While
the writing of a novel to show how the job should have been
done is something of a compliment, Moore also wrote scorn-
fully of Hardy's style both before and after *Tess* in several
books, earning Hardy's resentment.

Robert Louis Stevenson had admired Hardy's earlier novels,
especially *A Pair of Blue Eyes* and *The Mayor of Casterbridge*,
but about *Tess* he seems to have agreed with Henry James, who
(perhaps envious of Hardy's success) referred sarcastically to
the 'good little Thomas Hardy' and said that Tess was 'vile'.
Hardy had his revenge for these affronts. One of his last poems,
written on his deathbed, savagely attacks Moore's con-
ceitedness; he once termed James and Stevenson the 'Osric and
Polonius of novelists'; and in his autobiography he implies that
the common opinion of James in literary circles is that he lacked
virility.

From the publication of *Far from the Madding Crowd* in
1874 Hardy was recognised as a premier English novelist, and
he was admired by George Gissing, whose novels approached
Hardy's realism but not his romantic evocations of feeling. The
primary impact of *Tess*, and of Hardy, upon fiction was in
the early part of the twentieth century. D. H. Lawrence found
Hardy's critical portrayals of morality, religion, and social
institutions inspiring, although he disliked what he considered
Hardy's pessimism, which causes his human figures to be

destroyed by social standards instead of failing before 'the un-fathomed moral forces of nature' like the tragic sufferers of Shakespeare and Sophocles (*Study of Thomas Hardy*, quoted in Casagrande's *Hardy's Influence on the Modern Novel*, 37). Lawrence further develops the mysticism that is implicit in *Tess*, seeing in the interactions between humans and nature both the poetry that Hardy did and also a terror of creative destruc-tiveness. Sexuality in Hardy is almost always a matter of instinct and affection, sometimes but not always in combination; in Lawrence, behaviour during the sexual act conveys the basic values of the partners, individual values which reflect societal and economic systems as well as religious and family backgrounds. Sex is the arena in which essential forces operate; a person's truths are seen to be in violent, insistent opposition to those of the partner. Love is a matter of contest and exploitation in a more metaphysical sense than in Hardy. The clearest, if most varied, set of oppositional love relationships are those of Ursula and Birken, and of Gudrun and Gerald, in *Women in Love*.

Peter Casagrande explains that Hardy's impact was both in the matter of style, as in Virginia Woolf's 'powerfully suggestive lyricism' (*Hardy's Influence on the Modern Novel*, 26), and integrity and courage of his insistence upon treading on pre-viously forbidden grounds of sexuality and social mores, as James Joyce came to realise when he found it impossible to find a publisher or printer brave enough to bring out *Dubliners* (ibid., 25).

Hardy's fiction falls within a large European manner of writing that includes Ibsen, Zola, and Dreiser — the point I con-ceive these writers have in common is that their narratives are based on details of ordinary life, presented in such a way as to emphasise the subordination of the human actors to external forces. Ibsen's Hedda Gabler suggests the crippling power of gender roles; Zola's *Germinal* shows miners crushed by the economic tyranny of the owners. In these works, as in Hardy's, the values apparently advanced by the authors are sympathetic to the individual, resulting in a tone at best melancholic, at strongest an outrage and bitterness at the way the universe is constituted.

· These writers, while sometimes called 'naturalistic' on account of this characteristic, modify the starkness of destruction by invoking a quality of spirit in the protagonists in the course of their efforts to understand their situations, to isolate an identity that will give them a measure of dignity, to give a more special meaning to their existence than the mundaneness and even sordidness that surround them. Hardy, in comparison with these writers of similar perspective, offers more characters with sensitivity and awareness of the beauties of nature, and consequently he creates his peculiarly poignant moments when the reader realises that characters' finer qualities do not protect them from the inexorable operation of natural and social forces.

In discussing Hardy and Dreiser, Casagrande points out that 'Dreiser's admiration for Hardy . . . was part of a national [i.e., American] response', that William Dean Howells, Ellen Glasgow, Willa Cather, Hamlin Garland, and others responded to the Wessex Novels as well (Casagrande, *Hardy's Influence on the Modern Novel*, 173). In good part, Casagrande suggests, the response of several of these writers was owing to Hardy's qualities as a regional novelist, which appealed to the Americans wishing to make universal comments from their self-judged parochial knowledge – from Anderson's Winesburg, Ohio, and Ellen Glasgow's post-Civil War American South, to Cather's and Garland's rugged American Midwest being settled as the frontier moved further west. They held various views on Hardy's 'pessimism', which seemed to despair of the idea that humans could control or alleviate their suffering. Dreiser was in tune with Hardy's thinking in this regard. The presence of *Tess* in the sexual 'ruin' of Carrie in *Sister Carrie* is as unmistakable as it is in *Esther Waters*, with a reluctance on Dreiser's part similar to Moore's to have his heroine be destroyed by seduction. Instead, Carrie goes from her seducer to George Hurstwood, who in his ineffectuality when deprived of his position and money becomes the principal sufferer, resembling in his suicide Michael Henchard's asking that no one mourn or remember him. *Tess* plays a more dominant role in *Jennie Gerhardt*, the plot of which is practically a reprise of Hardy's story, the differences being that Jennie survives both of her seducers and does not suffer from Tess's self-guilt. Dreiser's heroines, like Moore's, are survivors in a world whose forces do not present sufferings greater than they can handle. For these novelists, self-preservation is a greater value than self-identity.

Peter Casagrande and John Rabbetts trace in detail some of Hardy's influences upon and affinities with such writers as John Cowper Powys, John Fowles, Faulkner, and others I discuss above. I have taken much from Casagrande in particular, sometimes attributing direct indebtedness, but not attempting to isolate those points on which my opinion differ from his. (Thus he should not be thought accountable for the picture here of Hardy's influence.)

Tess is by consensus Hardy's greatest work, its title character his single finest creation. Part of the justification for such judgements are the revisions and redactions of Tess's story in novels since 1890, as in some of those I have discussed here briefly. But it should not be thought that *Tess* is in itself totally a creation of the imagination that also created Wessex. Hardy himself had precursors – as varied as George Eliot's *Adam Bede*, Sir Walter Scott's *The Heart of Midlothian*, and particularly Gustave Flaubert's *Madame Bovary*. Indeed, Samuel Richardson's *Clarissa Harlowe* is unmistakably a predecessor. What makes *Tess* stand out in this line of novels presenting, and in effect analysing, a woman's loss of 'virtue', are its mingling of an often lyrical style and a romantic and even melodramatic plot, enwrapped by an authorial philosophy that permeates the narrative with a melancholy fury directed at the ultimate powers that shape existence for human beings. Capping the novel's unique quality is the quite evident infatuation of the author with his heroine – not in the sense that she is necessarily modelled on an actual person, but that in this combination of innocence, courage, wilfulness, and vitality Hardy has developed an inexhaustible object for his attention.

Further reading

This scholarship and literature on Hardy and on *Tess of the d Urbervilles* are immense in bulk, and generally of high quality. In important ways the novel evades anything approaching a final definition (as is the way with most great writing), but its materials – plot, characters, ideas – respond well to a variety of concerns. Some of these I have attempted to employ in this study, such as its reflection of literary concerns of its time (Richard Jefferies) and its utilisation of universal aesthetic principles (plot, as defined by Peter Brooks, in *Reading for the Plot: Design and Intention in Narrative* (Oxford: Clarendon Press, 1984)). Some of my comments on plot and tragedy reflect ideas from, if not the terminology of, such writers as Bakhtin (*The Dialogic Imagination: Four Essays by M. M. Bakhtin*, ed. Michael Holquist, trans. Caryl Emerson and Michael Holquist (Austin: University of Texas Press, 1981)).

Criticisms and analyses of the novel which I have especially benefited from and which may be more or less reflected in the present volume, although I do not always agree with their conclusions and hypotheses, include Albert Guerard, *Thomas Hardy: The Novels and Stories* (Cambridge, Mass.: Harvard University Press, 1949); Michael Millgate, *Thomas Hardy: His Career as a Novelist* (Oxford: Basil Blackwell, 1971); J. Hillis Miller, *Thomas Hardy: Distance and Desire* (Cambridge, Mass.: Harvard University Press, 1970); Penny Boumelha, *Thomas Hardy and Women: Sexual Ideology and Narrative Form* (Brighton: Harvester Press, 1982); Roy Morrell, *Thomas Hardy: The Will and the Way* (1965; rpt Oxford: Oxford University Press, 1978); and the chapter 'On *Tess of the d'Urbervilles*' in Dorothy Van Ghent, *The English Novel: Form and Function* (New York: Holt, Rinehart and Winston, 1953).

In the chapter on 'Backgrounds' I discuss Arnold Kettle's placing *Tess* within a class perspective. His first essay is in *An Introduction to the English Novel*, II: *Henry James to the Present* (London: Hutchinson, 1951), 49–62; he modifies his position in the Introduction to a school edition of *Tess* (New York: Harper and Row, 1966), xii n. Two more recent Marxist–orientated critics with techniques and terminology more complex than Arnold Kettle's are George Wotton, whose *Thomas Hardy: Towards a Materialist Criticism* (Dublin: Gill and Macmillan, 1985) is the first book–length study based on recent

Marxist methods of analysis, and John Goode, *Thomas Hardy: The Offensive Truth* (Oxford: Basil Blackwell, 1988). Both of these books testify in their different ways that Hardy presents a recalcitrant subject to ideological critics. Wotton is too abstract and unempathetic, relying finally on the iteration of his basic principle, which involves the production of Hardy's novels by the relations within a class society; Goode labours to maintain an abstract level of generalisation, but ultimately recognises that Hardy is himself too specific to be congenial to the drawing of abstractions. Despite his own fondness for large schemes, this resistance seems to be the mark of Hardy, as an object of Marxist or of any other sort of distinction–obliterating theory.

In recent years Hardy has begun to compete with Henry James, William Faulkner, and Dostoevsky as a novelist whose works provide test cases against critics' theories about basic principles of fiction. Among recent works testing *Tess* in this manner are Gillian Beer, *Darwin's Plots: Evolutionary Narrative in Darwin, George Eliot and Nineteenth–Century Fiction* (London: Routledge and Kegan Paul, 1983); Philip Weinstein, *The Semantics of Desire: Changing Models of Identity from Dickens to Joyce* (Princeton: Princeton University Press, 1984); J. Hillis Miller, *Fiction and Repetition: Seven English Novels* (Cambridge, Mass.: Harvard University Press, 1982).

Many useful studies of *Tess* are journal articles. A few of the best: Robert C. Schweik, 'Moral Perspective in *Tess of the d'Urbervilles*', *College English*, 24 (1962), 14–18; Elliott B. Gose Jr, 'Psychic Evolution: Darwinism and Initiation in *Tess of the d'Urbervilles*', *Nineteenth–Century Fiction*, 18 (1963), 261–72; Tony Tanner, 'Colour and Movement in Hardy's *Tess of the d'Urbervilles*', *Critical Quarterly*, 10 (1968), 219–39; Jan B. Gordon, 'Origins, History, and the Reconstitution of Family: Tess's Journey', *English Literary History*, 43 (1976), 366–88; Kathleen Blake, 'Pure Tess: Hardy on Knowing a Woman', *Studies in English Literature 1500–1900*, 22 (1982), 689–705; Charlotte Thompson, 'Language and the Shape of Reality in *Tess of the d'Urbervilles*', *English Literary History*, 50 (1983), 729–62; and Kaja Silverman, 'History, Figuration and Female Subjectivity in *Tess of the d'Urbervilles*', *Novel*, 18 (1984), 5–28. While I do not agree with all the critical approaches of these essays, each enriches a reader's comprehension of Hardy's accomplishment. There are many other essays worth reading, but those given address major issues of recent or current concern.

Essays and studies of the evolution of the text of *Tess*, from the earliest identifiable drafts of the manuscript through the pencilled alterations written in the fly–leaf of Hardy's 'study copy', provide insights into what he intended to emphasise in the novel and, in some cases, to diminish emphases on. After Richard Little Purdy's detailed brief sketch in his *Thomas Hardy: a Bibliographical Study*

(Oxford: Clarendon Press, 1954), the first ambitious and reasonably accurate study, particularly of changes in the manuscript, is J. T. Laird's *The Shaping of 'Tess of the d'Urbervilles'* (Oxford: Clarendon Press, 1975). Previous textual scholarship on the novel and much new work culminate in the Clarendon Edition, ed. Juliet Grindle and Simon Gatrell (Oxford: Clarendon Press, 1983). Simon Gatrell's subsequent *Hardy the Creator: a Textual Biography* (Oxford: Clarendon Press, 1988) considers Hardy's revisions for this novel in the context of revisions for most of the other novels over his full career.

Work on Hardy's creative and revising methods have fairly well destroyed the old sense of Hardy as an unschooled and unself–critical prose writer. Even so, there have not been enough studies of his skill with language, and the three best ones preceded the textual scholarship. Morton Dauwen Zabel, 'Hardy in Defence of His Art: the Aesthetic of Incongruity', in the special Thomas Hardy issue of *The Southern Review*, 6 (1940), 125–49; Zabel was one of the first and perhaps still the best thinkers about Hardy's aesthetics. Zabel's title conveys his belief that, far from being naïve about art, Hardy was fully aware of the dichotomous tendencies of his temperament and expressed the 'central discordance' of his full vision without compromise, refusing either to resort to exhortation or to forego the tactics that exploited his 'natural lack of artistic sophistication'. John Holloway's chapter 'Hardy' in *The Victorian Sage* (London: Macmillan, 1953), 244–89, is a perceptive deduction of Hardy's philosophical positions from statements and situations in the novels. David Lodge's 'Tess, Nature, and the Voices of Hardy' in *The Language of Fiction: Essays in Criticism and Verbal Analysis of the English Novel* (London: Routledge and Kegan Paul, 1966), 164–88, brilliantly clarifies the narrator's various positions and views; and John Bayley, *An Essay on Hardy* (Cambridge: Cambridge University Press, 1978), elicits delicate connections between Hardy as creator and the narrated scenes and situations.

Modern biographers have done well with Hardy, both in relating the life to the fiction, and in revealing facts of his life which he tried to obscure in his own account of his life in two volumes published originally under the name of his second wife Florence (*The Early Life of Thomas Hardy* (London: Macmillan, 1928) and *The Later Years of Thomas Hardy* (London: Macmillan, 1930)), recently edited by Michael Millgate with Hardy's own title restored to it, *The Life and Work of Thomas Hardy* (Athens: University of Georgia Press, 1985). The best biography overall is Michael Millgate, *Thomas Hardy: a Biography* (Oxford: Oxford University Press, 1982); but Robert Gittings' two–volume work – *Young Thomas Hardy* (London: Heinemann, 1975) and *The Older Hardy* (London: Heinemann, 1978) – also should be consulted. Underlying these volumes and supplementing them are *The Collected Letters of Thomas Hardy*, ed. Richard Little Purdy and Michael Millgate, 7 volumes (Oxford: Clarendon Press, 1978–89). An author's notebooks often are useful for tracing interest in intellectual and social issues; the most useful editions of Hardy's notebooks are *The Literary Notebooks of Thomas Hardy*, ed. Lennart A. Björk (Göteborg: Acta Universitatis Gothoburgensis, 1974; a fuller edition is London: Macmillan, 1985), and Richard H. Taylor, *The Personal Notebooks of Thomas Hardy* (London: Macmillan, 1979). Hardy's occasional essays, including 'The Dorsetshire Labourer', are reprinted in *Thomas Hardy's Personal Writings*, ed. Harold Orel (London: Macmillan, 1967).

Owing to space, I am not able to refer here to many other relevant studies, but readers may find interesting the history of the critical reception of Hardy that constitutes my introduction to *Critical Essays on Thomas Hardy: the Novels* (Boston, Mass.: G. K. Hall, 1990), and the more detailed evaluation of several critical and scholarly contributions to Hardy studies in my 'Recent Studies in Thomas Hardy's Fiction, 1980–1986', *Dickens Studies Annual*, 17 (1988), 241–76. The contemporary reviews of Hardy I refer to may be found in *Thomas Hardy: the Critical Heritage*, ed. R. G. Cox (London: Routledge and Kegan Paul, 1970). The two recent books which treat of Hardy's influence on other writers are Peter J. Casagrande, *Hardy's Influence on the Modern Novel* (London: Macmillan, 1987), and John Rabbetts, *From Hardy to Faulkner: Wessex to Yoknapatawpha* (New York: St Martin's Press, 1989). Of particular interest to those interested in the social construct 'Thomas Hardy' and in the general impact of Hardy as seen in film and education as well as in literary criticism is Peter Widdowson, *Hardy in History: a Study in Literary Sociology* (London: Routledge, 1989).

Other works cited

Terence Cave, *Recognitions: a Study in Poetics*, Oxford: Clarendon Press, 1988.

Helen Garwood, *Thomas Hardy: an Illustration of the Philosophy of Schopenhauer*, Philadelphia: John C. Winston, 1911.

Lucien Goldmann, 'The Tragic Vision: the World', in Lionel Abel (ed.), *Moderns on Tragedy*, 271–95, Greenwich, Conn.: Fawcett, 1967.

Richard Heath, 'Peasant Life in Dorset' (*Golden Hours*, 1872); rpt in *The English Peasant: Studies: Historical, Local, and Biographic*, London: T. Fisher Unwin, 1893.

Richard Jefferies, *Hodge and His Masters*, 2 volumes, London: Smith, Elder, 1880.

The Story of My Heart: My Autobiography, London: Longmans, 1883; Duckworth, 1923.

W. J. Keith, *Regions of the Imagination: the Development of British Rural Fiction.* Toronto: University of Toronto Press, 1988.

'Thomas Hardy and the Literary Pilgrims', *Nineteenth–Century Fiction*, 24 (1969), 80–92.

John O. Lyons, 'The Chronology of *Tess of the d'Urbervilles*', *Thomas Hardy Yearbook*, 16 (1988), 23–8.

Richard Mabey (ed.), *Landscape with Figures: an Anthology of Richard Jefferies's Prose*, Harmondsworth: Penguin, 1983.

Bernard J. Paris, ' "A Confusion of Many Standards": Conflicting Value Systems in *Tess of the d'Urbervilles*', *Nineteenth–Century Fiction* , 24 (1969), 57–9.

S. B. Saul 1969; 1979 with corrections). *The Myth of the Great Depression, 1873–1896*, London: Macmillan, 1969; rpt Macmillan, 1979.

Max Keith Sutton, *R. D. Blackmore*. Boston, Mass.: Twayne, 1979.

Leon Waldoff, 'Psychological Determinism in *Tess*', in Dale Kramer (ed.), *Critical Approaches to the Fiction of Thomas Hardy*, 135–54, London: Macmillan, 1979.